Just The
facts101
Textbook Key Facts

Textbook Outlines, Highlights, and Practice Quizzes

Health Economics

by Jay Bhattacharya, 1 Edition

All "Just the Facts101" Material Written or Prepared by Cram101 Textbook Reviews

Title Page

facts101
LEARNING SYSTEM

"Just the Facts101" is a Content Technologies publication and tool designed to give you all the facts from your textbooks. Register for the full practice test for each of your chapters for virtually any of your textbooks.

Facts101 has built custom study tools specific to your textbook. We provide all of the factual testable information and unlike traditional study guides, we will never send you back to your textbook for more information.

YOU WILL NEVER HAVE TO HIGHLIGHT A BOOK AGAIN!

Facts101 StudyGuides

All of the information in this StudyGuide is written specifically for your textbook. We include the key terms, places, people, and concepts... the information you can expect on your next exam!

Facts101

Only Facts101 gives you the outlines, highlights, and PRACTICE TESTS specific to your textbook. Facts101 sister Cram101.com is an online application where you'll discover study tools designed to make the most of your limited study time.

www.Cram101.com

ISBN(s): 9781538839188. PUBI-2.2017211

STUDYING MADE EASY

This Craml0l notebook is designed to make studying easier and increase your comprehension of the textbook material. Instead of starting with a blank notebook and trying to write down everything discussed in class lectures, you can use this Craml0l textbook notebook and annotate your notes along with the lecture.

Our goal is to give you the best tools for success.

For a supreme understanding of the course, pair your notebook with our online tools at www.cram101.com

Our Online Access program is a simple way for us to keep our promise and provide you the best studying tools, regardless of where you purchased your Craml0l textbook notebook. As long as you let us know you are intereested in a free online access account we will set it up for you for 180 days.

Online Access:

facts101

Health Economics
Jay Bhattacharya, 1

CONTENTS

1. Why health economics?

CHAPTER OUTLINE: KEY TERMS, PEOPLE, PLACES, CONCEPTS

	CARE
	Health care
	Budget
	Economics
	Welfare
	Welfare economics

CHAPTER HIGHLIGHTS & NOTES: KEY TERMS, PEOPLE, PLACES, CONCEPTS

CARE	CARE is a major international humanitarian agency delivering broad-spectrum emergency relief and long-term international development projects. Founded in 1945, CARE is nonsectarian, non-partisan, and non-governmental. It is one of the largest and oldest humanitarian aid organizations focused on fighting global poverty.
Health care	Health care is the diagnosis, treatment, and prevention of disease, illness, injury, and other physical and mental impairments in human beings. Health care is delivered by practitioners in allied health, dentistry, midwifery-obstetrics, medicine, nursing, optometry, pharmacy, psychology and other care providers. It refers to the work done in providing primary care, secondary care, and tertiary care, as well as in public health.
Budget	A budget is a quantitative expression of a plan for a defined period of time. It may include planned sales volumes and revenues, resource quantities, costs and expenses, assets, liabilities and cash flows. It expresses strategic plans of business units, organizations, activities or events in measurable terms.
Economics	Economics is the social science that studies the behavior of individuals, households, and organizations, when they manage or use scarce resources, which have alternative uses, to achieve desired ends. Agents are assumed to act rationally, have multiple desirable ends in sight, limited resources to obtain these ends, a set of stable preferences, a definite overall guiding objective, and the capability of making a choice.

1. Why health economics?

Welfare	Welfare is the provision of a minimal level of well-being and social support for all citizens, sometimes referred to as public aid. In most developed countries welfare is largely provided by the government, and to a lesser extent, charities, informal social groups, religious groups, and inter-governmental organizations. The welfare state expands on this concept to include services such as universal healthcare and unemployment insurance.
Welfare economics	Welfare economics is a branch of economics that uses microeconomic techniques to evaluate well-being from allocation of productive factors as to desirability and economic efficiency within an economy, often relative to competitive general equilibrium. It analyzes social welfare, however measured, in terms of economic activities of the individuals that compose the theoretical society considered. Accordingly, individuals, with associated economic activities, are the basic units for aggregating to social welfare, whether of a group, a community, or a society, and there is no 'social welfare' apart from the 'welfare' associated with its individual units.

1. _____ is a major international humanitarian agency delivering broad-spectrum emergency relief and long-term international development projects. Founded in 1945, _____ is nonsectarian, non-partisan, and non-governmental. It is one of the largest and oldest humanitarian aid organizations focused on fighting global poverty.

   a. CARE
   b. Benevolent Organisation for Development, Health and Insight
   c. Bethlehem Association
   d. Beyond Sport

2. A _____ is a quantitative expression of a plan for a defined period of time. It may include planned sales volumes and revenues, resource quantities, costs and expenses, assets, liabilities and cash flows. It expresses strategic plans of business units, organizations, activities or events in measurable terms.

   a. Budget
   b. Fuel protests in the United Kingdom
   c. Battle of Annaberg
   d. Freikorps Lichtschlag

3. . _____ is the social science that studies the behavior of individuals, households, and organizations, when they manage or use scarce resources, which have alternative uses, to achieve desired ends.

Agents are assumed to act rationally, have multiple desirable ends in sight, limited resources to obtain these ends, a set of stable preferences, a definite overall guiding objective, and the capability of making a choice. There exists an _____(s) problem, subject to study by _____(s) science, when a decision (choice) has to be made by one or more resource-controlling players to attain the best possible outcome under bounded rational conditions.

a. Critical minimum effort theory
b. Swedish Academy
c. Economics
d. Boston Stock Exchange

4. _____ is the diagnosis, treatment, and prevention of disease, illness, injury, and other physical and mental impairments in human beings. _____ is delivered by practitioners in allied health, dentistry, midwifery-obstetrics, medicine, nursing, optometry, pharmacy, psychology and other care providers. It refers to the work done in providing primary care, secondary care, and tertiary care, as well as in public health.

a. Spindletop
b. Health care
c. Bethlehem Association
d. Beyond Sport

5. _____ is the provision of a minimal level of well-being and social support for all citizens, sometimes referred to as public aid. In most developed countries _____ is largely provided by the government, and to a lesser extent, charities, informal social groups, religious groups, and inter-governmental organizations.

The _____ state expands on this concept to include services such as universal healthcare and unemployment insurance.

a. Fuel protests in the United Kingdom
b. Welfare
c. Freikorps Lichtschlag
d. Freikorps Oberland

1. a

2. a

3. c

4. b

5. b

You can take the complete Online Interactive Chapter Practice Test

for 1. Why health economics?
on all key terms, persons, places, and concepts.

No Additional Costs

http://www.Cram101.com

Register, send an email request to Travis.Reese@Cram101.com to get your user Id and password.

Include your customer order number, and ISBN number from your studyguide Retailer.

2. Demand for health care

_____ | Delphi

_____ | CARE

_____ | Demand

_____ | Health care

_____ | Health insurance

_____ | Insurance

_____ | Budget

_____ | Medicaid

_____ | RAND Health Insurance Experiment

_____ | Orphan drug

_____ | Tropical disease

_____ | Emergency

_____ | China

_____ | Medicare

_____ | Elasticity

_____ | Prescription

_____ | Price

_____ | Price elasticity

_____ | Trust

2. Demand for health care

Delphi	Delphi Forums is a former U.S. online service provider and since the mid 1990s has been a community internet forum site. It started as a nationwide dialup service in 1983. Delphi Forums remains active as of 2013, claiming 4 million registered members and 'more than 8,000 active Forums'.
CARE	CARE is a major international humanitarian agency delivering broad-spectrum emergency relief and long-term international development projects. Founded in 1945, CARE is nonsectarian, non-partisan, and non-governmental. It is one of the largest and oldest humanitarian aid organizations focused on fighting global poverty.
Demand	In economics, demand for a good or service is an entire listing of the quantity of the good or service that a market would choose to buy, for every possible market price of the good or service. (Note: This distinguishes 'demand' from 'quantity demanded', where demand is a listing or graphing of quantity demanded at each possible price. In contrast to demand, quantity demanded is the exact quantity demanded at a certain price.
Health care	Health care is the diagnosis, treatment, and prevention of disease, illness, injury, and other physical and mental impairments in human beings. Health care is delivered by practitioners in allied health, dentistry, midwifery-obstetrics, medicine, nursing, optometry, pharmacy, psychology and other care providers. It refers to the work done in providing primary care, secondary care, and tertiary care, as well as in public health.
Health insurance	Health insurance is insurance against the risk of incurring medical expenses among individuals. By estimating the overall risk of health care and health system expenses, among a targeted group, an insurer can develop a routine finance structure, such as a monthly premium or payroll tax, to ensure that money is available to pay for the health care benefits specified in the insurance agreement. The benefit is administered by a central organization such as a government agency, private business, or not-for-profit entity.
Insurance	Insurance is the equitable transfer of the risk of a loss, from one entity to another in exchange for payment. It is a form of risk management primarily used to hedge against the risk of a contingent, uncertain loss. According to study texts of The Chartered Insurance Institute, there are the following categories of risk:•Financial risks which means that the risk must have financial measurement.•Pure risks which means that the risk must be real and not related to gambling•Particular risks which means that these risks are not widespread in their effect, for example such as earthquake risk for the region prone to it. It is commonly accepted that only financial, pure and particular risks are insurable.
Budget	A budget is a quantitative expression of a plan for a defined period of time.

2. Demand for health care

	It may include planned sales volumes and revenues, resource quantities, costs and expenses, assets, liabilities and cash flows. It expresses strategic plans of business units, organizations, activities or events in measurable terms.
Medicaid	Medicaid in the United States is a social health care program for families and individuals with low income and resources. The Health Insurance Association of America describes Medicaid as a 'government insurance program for persons of all ages whose income and resources are insufficient to pay for health care.' (America's Health Insurance Plans (HIAA), pg. 232). Medicaid is the largest source of funding for medical and health-related services for people with low income in the United States.
RAND Health Insurance Experiment	The RAND Health Insurance Experiment was an experimental study of health care costs, utilization and outcomes in the United States, which assigned people randomly to different kinds of plans and followed their behavior, from 1974 to 1982. As a result, it provided stronger evidence than studies that examine people afterwards who were not randomly assigned. It concluded that cost sharing reduced 'inappropriate or unnecessary' medical care (overutilization), but also reduced 'appropriate or needed' medical care. It did not have enough statistical power to tell whether people who got less appropriate or needed care were more likely to die as a result.
Orphan drug	An orphan drug is a pharmaceutical agent that has been developed specifically to treat a rare medical condition, the condition itself being referred to as an orphan disease. In the US and EU it is easier to gain marketing approval for an orphan drug, and there may be other financial incentives, such as extended exclusivity periods, all intended to encourage the development of drugs which might otherwise lack a sufficient profit motive. The assignment of orphan status to a disease and to any drugs developed to treat it is a matter of public policy in many countries, and has resulted in medical breakthroughs that may not have otherwise been achieved due to the economics of drug research and development.
Tropical disease	Tropical diseases are diseases that are prevalent in or unique to tropical and subtropical regions. The diseases are less prevalent in temperate climates, due in part to the occurrence of a cold season, which controls the insect population by forcing hibernation. Insects such as mosquitoes and flies are by far the most common disease carrier, or vector.
Emergency	Emergency is a humanitarian NGO that provides emergency medical treatment to civilian victims of war, especially in relation to landmines. It was founded by war surgeon Gino Strada in 1994 in Milan (Italy). Gino Strada and the other founders of Emergency aimed to bring free, high-quality medical and surgical assistance to war victims.
China	China, officially the People's Republic of China, is a sovereign state located in East Asia. It is the world's most populous country, with a population of over 1.35 billion.

2. Demand for health care

Medicare	In the United States, Medicare is a national social insurance program, administered by the U.S. federal government since 1966, that guarantees access to health insurance for Americans aged 65 and older who have worked and paid into the system, and younger people with disabilities as well as people with end stage renal disease (Medicare.gov, 2012) and persons with amyotrophic lateral sclerosis. As a social insurance program, Medicare spreads the financial risk associated with illness across society to protect everyone, and thus has a somewhat different social role from for-profit private insurers, which manage their risk portfolio by adjusting their pricing according to perceived risk. In 2010, Medicare provided health insurance to 48 million Americans--40 million people age 65 and older and eight million younger people with disabilities.
Elasticity	In economics, elasticity is the measurement of how responsive an economic variable is to a change in another. For example:•'If I lower the price of my product, how much more will I sell?'•'If I raise the price of one good, how will that affect sales of this other good?'•'If we learn that a resource is becoming scarce, will people scramble to acquire it?' An elastic variable (or elasticity value greater than 1) is one which responds more than proportionally to changes in other variables. In contrast, an inelastic variable (or elasticity value less than 1) is one which changes less than proportionally in response to changes in other variables.
Prescription	In law, prescription is the method of sovereignty transfer of a territory through international law analogous to the common law doctrine of adverse possession for private real-estate. Prescription involves the open encroachment by the new sovereign upon the territory in question for a prolonged period of time, acting as the sovereign, without protest or other contest by the original sovereign. This doctrine legalizes de jure the de facto transfer of sovereignty caused in part by the original sovereign's extended negligence and/or neglect of the area in question.
Price	In ordinary usage, price is the quantity of payment or compensation given by one party to another in return for goods or services. In modern economies, prices are generally expressed in units of some form of currency. (For commodities, they are expressed as currency per unit weight of the commodity, e.g. euros per kilogram).
Price elasticity	Price elasticity of demand is a measure used in economics to show the responsiveness, or elasticity, of the quantity demanded of a good or service to a change in its price. More precisely, it gives the percentage change in quantity demanded in response to a one percent change in price (ceteris paribus, i.e. holding constant all the other determinants of demand, such as income).

2. Demand for health care

Trust	A 'trust,' or 'corporate trust' means a large business. Originally, it was Standard Oil, which was already the largest corporation in the world

1. In economics, _____ for a good or service is an entire listing of the quantity of the good or service that a market would choose to buy, for every possible market price of the good or service. (Note: This distinguishes '_____' from 'quantity demanded', where _____ is a listing or graphing of quantity demanded at each possible price. In contrast to _____, quantity demanded is the exact quantity demanded at a certain price.

    a. Budget set
    b. Demand
    c. Consumer service
    d. Consumption

2. _____ Forums is a former U.S. online service provider and since the mid 1990s has been a community internet forum site. It started as a nationwide dialup service in 1983. _____ Forums remains active as of 2013, claiming 4 million registered members and 'more than 8,000 active Forums'.

    a. C.mmp
    b. Calculus ratiocinator
    c. Delphi
    d. Computer Conservation Society

3. _____ is a humanitarian NGO that provides _____ medical treatment to civilian victims of war, especially in relation to landmines. It was founded by war surgeon Gino Strada in 1994 in Milan (Italy).

    Gino Strada and the other founders of _____ aimed to bring free, high-quality medical and surgical assistance to war victims.

    a. Bah%C3%A1%27%C3%AD International Community
    b. Benevolent Organisation for Development, Health and Insight
    c. Emergency
    d. Beyond Sport

4. . In economics, _____ is the measurement of how responsive an economic variable is to a change in another. For example:•'If I lower the price of my product, how much more will I sell?'•'If I raise the price of one good, how will that affect sales of this other good?'•'If we learn that a resource is becoming scarce, will people scramble to acquire it?'

An elastic variable (or _____ value greater than 1) is one which responds more than proportionally to changes in other variables. In contrast, an inelastic variable (or _____ value less than 1) is one which changes less than proportionally in response to changes in other variables.

a. Benefit principle
b. Bliss point
c. Club good
d. Elasticity

5. _____ is a major international humanitarian agency delivering broad-spectrum emergency relief and long-term international development projects. Founded in 1945, _____ is nonsectarian, non-partisan, and non-governmental. It is one of the largest and oldest humanitarian aid organizations focused on fighting global poverty.

a. Bah%C3%A1%27%C3%AD International Community
b. Benevolent Organisation for Development, Health and Insight
c. CARE
d. Beyond Sport

1. b
2. c
3. c
4. d
5. c

You can take the complete Online Interactive Chapter Practice Test

for 2. Demand for health care
on all key terms, persons, places, and concepts.

No Additional Costs

http://www.Cram101.com

Register, send an email request to Travis.Reese@Cram101.com to get your user Id and password.

Include your customer order number, and ISBN number from your studyguide Retailer.

3. Demand for health: the Grossman model

Budget

Consumption

Good

Utility

Production

Budget constraint

Market

Capital

Indifference curve

Cuba

CARE

Demand

Efficiency

Investment

Comparative statics

Gradient

Hypothesis

3. Demand for health: the Grossman model

Budget	A budget is a quantitative expression of a plan for a defined period of time. It may include planned sales volumes and revenues, resource quantities, costs and expenses, assets, liabilities and cash flows. It expresses strategic plans of business units, organizations, activities or events in measurable terms.
Consumption	Consumption is a major concept in economics and is also studied by many other social sciences. Economists are particularly interested in the relationship between consumption and income, and therefore in economics the consumption function plays a major role. Different schools of economists define production and consumption differently.
Good	In economics, a good is a material that satisfies human wants and provides utility, for example, to a consumer making a purchase. A common distinction is made between 'goods' that are tangible property (also called goods) and services, which are non-physical. Commodities may be used as a synonym for economic goods but often refer to marketable raw materials and primary products.
Utility	Utility, or usefulness, is the ability of something to satisfy needs or wants. Utility is an important concept in economics and game theory, because it represents satisfaction experienced by the consumer of a good. Not coincidentally, a good is something that satisfies human wants and provides utility, for example, to a consumer making a purchase.
Production	Production is a process of combining various material inputs and immaterial inputs in order to make something for consumption (the output). It is the act of creating output, a good or service which has value and contributes to the utility of individuals. Economic well-being is created in a production process, meaning all economic activities that aim directly or indirectly to satisfy human needs.
Budget constraint	A budget constraint represents all the combinations of goods and services that a consumer may purchase given current prices within his or her given income. Consumer theory uses the concepts of a budget constraint and a preference map to analyze consumer choices. Both concepts have a ready graphical representation in the two-good case.
Market	A market is one of the many varieties of systems, institutions, procedures, social relations and infrastructures whereby parties engage in exchange. While parties may exchange goods and services by barter, most markets rely on sellers offering their goods or services (including labor) in exchange for money from buyers. It can be said that a market is the process by which the prices of goods and services are established.
Capital	In economics, capital goods, real capital, or capital assets are already-produced durable goods or any non-financial asset that is used in production of goods or services. Capital goods are not significantly consumed in the production process though they may depreciate.

3. Demand for health: the Grossman model

Indifference curve	In microeconomic theory, an indifference curve is a graph showing different bundles of goods between which a consumer is indifferent. That is, at each point on the curve, the consumer has no preference for one bundle over another. One can equivalently refer to each point on the indifference curve as rendering the same level of utility (satisfaction) for the consumer.
Cuba	Cuba, officially the Republic of Cuba is an island country in the Caribbean. The nation of Cuba comprises the main island of Cuba, the Isla de la Juventud, and several archipelagos. Havana is the capital of Cuba and its largest city.
CARE	CARE is a major international humanitarian agency delivering broad-spectrum emergency relief and long-term international development projects. Founded in 1945, CARE is nonsectarian, non-partisan, and non-governmental. It is one of the largest and oldest humanitarian aid organizations focused on fighting global poverty.
Demand	In economics, demand for a good or service is an entire listing of the quantity of the good or service that a market would choose to buy, for every possible market price of the good or service. (Note: This distinguishes 'demand' from 'quantity demanded', where demand is a listing or graphing of quantity demanded at each possible price. In contrast to demand, quantity demanded is the exact quantity demanded at a certain price.
Efficiency	Efficiency in general, describes the extent to which time, effort or cost is well used for the intended task or purpose. It is often used with the specific purpose of relaying the capability of a specific application of effort to produce a specific outcome effectively with a minimum amount or quantity of waste, expense, or unnecessary effort. 'Efficiency' has widely varying meanings in different disciplines.
Investment	Investment is time, energy, or matter spent in the hope of future benefits. Investment has different meanings in economics and finance. In economics, investment is the accumulation of newly produced physical entities, such as factories, machinery, houses, and goods inventories.
Comparative statics	In economics, comparative statics is the comparison of two different economic outcomes, before and after a change in some underlying exogenous parameter. As a study of statics it compares two different equilibrium states, after the process of adjustment . It does not study the motion towards equilibrium, nor the process of the change itself.
Gradient	In mathematics, the gradient is a generalization of the usual concept of derivative of a function in one dimension to a function in several dimensions. If $f(x_1, .. x_n)$ is a differentiable, scalar-valued function of standard Cartesian coordinates in Euclidean space, its gradient is the vector whose components are the n partial derivatives of f.

| Hypothesis | A hypothesis is a proposed explanation for a phenomenon. For a hypothesis to be a scientific hypothesis, the scientific method requires that one can test it. Scientists generally base scientific hypotheses on previous observations that cannot satisfactorily be explained with the available scientific theories. |

1. A _____ is a quantitative expression of a plan for a defined period of time. It may include planned sales volumes and revenues, resource quantities, costs and expenses, assets, liabilities and cash flows. It expresses strategic plans of business units, organizations, activities or events in measurable terms.

   a. Rachel Ashwell
   b. Budget
   c. Battle of Annaberg
   d. Freikorps Lichtschlag

2. _____, officially the Republic of _____ is an island country in the Caribbean. The nation of _____ comprises the main island of _____, the Isla de la Juventud, and several archipelagos. Havana is the capital of _____ and its largest city.

   a. Central Asian-American Enterprise Fund
   b. Cuba
   c. Sino-Soviet split
   d. Fuel protests in the United Kingdom

3. In economics, _____ is the comparison of two different economic outcomes, before and after a change in some underlying exogenous parameter.

   As a study of statics it compares two different equilibrium states, after the process of adjustment . It does not study the motion towards equilibrium, nor the process of the change itself.

   a. Comparative statics
   b. Battle of Annaberg
   c. Freikorps Lichtschlag
   d. Freikorps Oberland

4. . _____ is a major concept in economics and is also studied by many other social sciences. Economists are particularly interested in the relationship between _____ and income, and therefore in economics the _____ function plays a major role.

3. Demand for health: the Grossman model

Different schools of economists define production and _____ differently.

a. Budget set
b. Consumption
c. Consumer service
d. Fuel protests in the United Kingdom

5. In mathematics, the _____ is a generalization of the usual concept of derivative of a function in one dimension to a function in several dimensions. If $f(x_1, .. x_n)$ is a differentiable, scalar-valued function of standard Cartesian coordinates in Euclidean space, its _____ is the vector whose components are the n partial derivatives of f. It is thus a vector-valued function.

a. Spindletop
b. Battle of Annaberg
c. Freikorps Lichtschlag
d. Gradient

1. b
2. b
3. a
4. b
5. d

You can take the complete Online Interactive Chapter Practice Test

for 3. Demand for health: the Grossman model
on all key terms, persons, places, and concepts.

No Additional Costs

http://www.Cram101.com

Register, send an email request to Travis.Reese@Cram101.com to get your user Id and password.

Include your customer order number, and ISBN number from your studyguide Retailer.

CHAPTER OUTLINE: KEY TERMS, PEOPLE, PLACES, CONCEPTS

	Cuba
	Demand
	Hypothesis
	Income
	Income inequality
	Status
	Index
	Gradient
	Health insurance
	Insurance
	China
	Capital
	Efficiency
	Chernobyl disaster
	Natural experiment
	Screening
	Price
	Adverse selection
	CARE
	Medicaid
	Retirement

4. Socioeconomic disparities in health

	Access
	Child mortality
	Medicare
	Delayed gratification
	Preference
	Time preference
	Theory

CHAPTER HIGHLIGHTS & NOTES: KEY TERMS, PEOPLE, PLACES, CONCEPTS

Cuba	Cuba, officially the Republic of Cuba is an island country in the Caribbean. The nation of Cuba comprises the main island of Cuba, the Isla de la Juventud, and several archipelagos. Havana is the capital of Cuba and its largest city.
Demand	In economics, demand for a good or service is an entire listing of the quantity of the good or service that a market would choose to buy, for every possible market price of the good or service. (Note: This distinguishes 'demand' from 'quantity demanded', where demand is a listing or graphing of quantity demanded at each possible price. In contrast to demand, quantity demanded is the exact quantity demanded at a certain price.
Hypothesis	A hypothesis is a proposed explanation for a phenomenon. For a hypothesis to be a scientific hypothesis, the scientific method requires that one can test it. Scientists generally base scientific hypotheses on previous observations that cannot satisfactorily be explained with the available scientific theories.
Income	Income is the consumption and savings opportunity gained by an entity within a specified timeframe, which is generally expressed in monetary terms. However, for households and individuals, 'income is the sum of all the wages, salaries, profits, interests payments, rents and other forms of earnings received... in a given period of time.'

	In the field of public economics, the term may refer to the accumulation of both monetary and non-monetary consumption ability, with the former (monetary) being used as a proxy for total income.
Income inequality	Economic inequality (also described as the gap between rich and poor, income inequality, wealth disparity, wealth and income differences or wealth gap) is the state of affairs in which assets, wealth, or income are distributed unequally among individuals in a group, among groups in a population, or among countries. The issue of economic inequality can implicate notions of equity, equality of outcome, equality of opportunity, and even life expectancy. Although the phrase uses the term income, the discussion often includes inequality in wealth or assets, which are different concepts.
Status	An Individual's status is a legal position held in regards to the rest of the community and not by an act of law or by the consensual acts of the parties, and it is in rem, i.e. these conditions must be recognised by the world. It is the qualities of universality and permanence that distinguish status from consensual relationships such as employment and agency. Hence, a person's status and its attributes are set by the law of the domicile if born in a common law state, or by the law of nationality if born in a civil law state and this status and its attendant capacities should be recognised wherever the person may later travel.
Index	In economics and finance, an index is a statistical measure of changes in a representative group of individual data points. These data may be derived from any number of sources, including company performance, prices, productivity, and employment. Economic indices (index, plural) track economic health from different perspectives.
Gradient	In mathematics, the gradient is a generalization of the usual concept of derivative of a function in one dimension to a function in several dimensions. If $f(x_1, .. x_n)$ is a differentiable, scalar-valued function of standard Cartesian coordinates in Euclidean space, its gradient is the vector whose components are the n partial derivatives of f. It is thus a vector-valued function.
Health insurance	Health insurance is insurance against the risk of incurring medical expenses among individuals. By estimating the overall risk of health care and health system expenses, among a targeted group, an insurer can develop a routine finance structure, such as a monthly premium or payroll tax, to ensure that money is available to pay for the health care benefits specified in the insurance agreement. The benefit is administered by a central organization such as a government agency, private business, or not-for-profit entity.
Insurance	Insurance is the equitable transfer of the risk of a loss, from one entity to another in exchange for payment. It is a form of risk management primarily used to hedge against the risk of a contingent, uncertain loss.

4. Socioeconomic disparities in health

	According to study texts of The Chartered Insurance Institute, there are the following categories of risk:•Financial risks which means that the risk must have financial measurement.•Pure risks which means that the risk must be real and not related to gambling•Particular risks which means that these risks are not widespread in their effect, for example such as earthquake risk for the region prone to it. It is commonly accepted that only financial, pure and particular risks are insurable.
China	China, officially the People's Republic of China, is a sovereign state located in East Asia. It is the world's most populous country, with a population of over 1.35 billion. The PRC is a single-party state governed by the Communist Party, with its seat of government in the capital city of Beijing.
Capital	In economics, capital goods, real capital, or capital assets are already-produced durable goods or any non-financial asset that is used in production of goods or services. Capital goods are not significantly consumed in the production process though they may depreciate. How a capital good or is maintained or returned to its pre-production state varies with the type of capital involved.
Efficiency	Efficiency in general, describes the extent to which time, effort or cost is well used for the intended task or purpose. It is often used with the specific purpose of relaying the capability of a specific application of effort to produce a specific outcome effectively with a minimum amount or quantity of waste, expense, or unnecessary effort. 'Efficiency' has widely varying meanings in different disciplines.
Chernobyl disaster	The Chernobyl disaster was a catastrophic nuclear accident that occurred on 26 April 1986 at the Chernobyl Nuclear Power Plant in Ukraine (then officially the Ukrainian SSR), which was under the direct jurisdiction of the central authorities of the Soviet Union. An explosion and fire released large quantities of radioactive particles into the atmosphere, which spread over much of the western USSR and Europe. The Chernobyl disaster is the worst nuclear power plant accident in history in terms of cost and resulting deaths, and is one of only two classified as a level 7 event (the maximum classification) on the International Nuclear Event Scale (the other being the Fukushima Daiichi nuclear disaster in 2011).
Natural experiment	A natural experiment is an empirical study in which individuals exposed to the experimental and control conditions are determined by nature or by other factors outside the control of the investigators, yet the process governing the exposures arguably resembles random assignment. Thus, natural experiments are observational studies and are not controlled in the traditional sense of a randomized experiment.

Screening	Screening in economics refers to a strategy of combating adverse selection, one of the potential decision-making complications in cases of asymmetric information. The concept of screening was first developed by Michael Spence (1973), and should be distinguished from signalling, which implies that the informed agent moves first.
	For purposes of screening, asymmetric information cases assume two economic agents--which we call, for example, Abel and Cain--where Abel knows more about himself than Cain knows about Abel.
Price	In ordinary usage, price is the quantity of payment or compensation given by one party to another in return for goods or services.
	In modern economies, prices are generally expressed in units of some form of currency. (For commodities, they are expressed as currency per unit weight of the commodity, e.g. euros per kilogram).
Adverse selection	Adverse selection, anti-selection, or negative selection is a term used in economics, insurance, risk management, and statistics. It refers to a market process in which undesired results occur when buyers and sellers have asymmetric information (access to different information); the 'bad' products or services are more likely to be selected. For example, a bank that sets one price for all of its checking account customers runs the risk of being adversely selected against by its low-balance, high-activity (and hence least profitable) customers.
CARE	CARE is a major international humanitarian agency delivering broad-spectrum emergency relief and long-term international development projects. Founded in 1945, CARE is nonsectarian, non-partisan, and non-governmental. It is one of the largest and oldest humanitarian aid organizations focused on fighting global poverty.
Medicaid	Medicaid in the United States is a social health care program for families and individuals with low income and resources. The Health Insurance Association of America describes Medicaid as a 'government insurance program for persons of all ages whose income and resources are insufficient to pay for health care.' (America's Health Insurance Plans (HIAA), pg. 232). Medicaid is the largest source of funding for medical and health-related services for people with low income in the United States.
Retirement	Retirement is the point where a person stops employment completely. A person may also semi-retire by reducing work hours.
	Many people choose to retire when they are eligible for private or public pension benefits, although some are forced to retire when physical conditions no longer allow the person to work any more (by illness or accident) or as a result of legislation concerning their position.

4. Socioeconomic disparities in health

Access	Access is a catalytic process that enables interactions, contact and exchanges among people, businesses and nations. An analytical framework to define the drivers and benefits of Access and to quantify the impact of Access on economic growth and personal well-being was created in 2006 by the Center for Science, Technology, and Economic Development at SRI International (formerly known as the Stanford Research Institute) in its study, "The Power of Access" (also titled, "How Greater Access Is Changing The World: A Landmark Study on the Relevance of Access to People, Businesses and Nations"). As outlined in the study, the Access framework consists of the Access Model, which expresses the function of Access as an econometric equation; the "Access Cycle"; and the 'Access Index,' which ranks 75 nations based on their performance in 22 metrics, including transportation infrastructure; telecommunications networks; trade policy; and news, media and information services.
Child mortality	Child mortality, also known as under-5 mortality, refers to the death of infants and children under the age of five. In 2012, 6.6 million, 2011, 6.9 million children under five died, down from 7.6 million in 2010, 8.1 million in 2009, and 12.4 million in 1990. About half of child deaths occur in Sub-Saharan Africa. Reduction of child mortality is the fourth of the United Nations' Millennium Development Goals. Child Mortality Rate is the highest in low-income countries, such as most countries in Sub-Saharan Africa. A child's death is emotionally and physically damaging for the mourning parents.
Medicare	In the United States, Medicare is a national social insurance program, administered by the U.S. federal government since 1966, that guarantees access to health insurance for Americans aged 65 and older who have worked and paid into the system, and younger people with disabilities as well as people with end stage renal disease (Medicare.gov, 2012) and persons with amyotrophic lateral sclerosis. As a social insurance program, Medicare spreads the financial risk associated with illness across society to protect everyone, and thus has a somewhat different social role from for-profit private insurers, which manage their risk portfolio by adjusting their pricing according to perceived risk. In 2010, Medicare provided health insurance to 48 million Americans--40 million people age 65 and older and eight million younger people with disabilities.
Delayed gratification	Delayed gratification, or deferred gratification, is the ability to resist the temptation for an immediate reward and wait for a later reward. Generally, delayed gratification is associated with resisting a smaller but more immediate reward in order to receive a larger or more enduring reward later. A growing body of literature has linked the ability to delay gratification to a host of other positive outcomes, including academic success, physical health, psychological health, and social competence.

Preference	In economics and other social sciences, preference refers to the set of assumptions related to ordering some alternatives, based on the degree of happiness, satisfaction, gratification, enjoyment, or utility they provide, a process which results in an optimal 'choice' . Although economists are usually not interested in choices or preferences in themselves, they are interested in the theory of choice because it serves as a background for empirical demand analysis.
Time preference	In economics, time preference is the relative valuation placed on a good at an earlier date compared with its valuation at a later date. There is no absolute distinction that separates 'high' and 'low' time preference, only comparisons with others either individually or in aggregate. Someone with a high time preference is focused substantially on his well-being in the present and the immediate future relative to the average person, while someone with low time preference places more emphasis than average on their well-being in the further future.
Theory	Theory is a group of ideas meant to explain a certain topic of science, such as a single or collection of fact, event(s), or phenomen(a)(on). Typically, a theory is developed through the use of contemplative and rational forms of abstract and generalized thinking. Furthermore, a theory is often based on general principles that are independent of the thing being explained.

1. In economics, _____ for a good or service is an entire listing of the quantity of the good or service that a market would choose to buy, for every possible market price of the good or service. (Note: This distinguishes '_____' from 'quantity demanded', where _____ is a listing or graphing of quantity demanded at each possible price. In contrast to _____, quantity demanded is the exact quantity demanded at a certain price.

   a. Demand
   b. Complementary good
   c. Consumer service
   d. Consumption

2. . _____ is a major international humanitarian agency delivering broad-spectrum emergency relief and long-term international development projects. Founded in 1945, _____ is nonsectarian, non-partisan, and non-governmental. It is one of the largest and oldest humanitarian aid organizations focused on fighting global poverty.

   a. Bah%C3%A1%27%C3%AD International Community
   b. Benevolent Organisation for Development, Health and Insight
   c. Bethlehem Association

4. Socioeconomic disparities in health

3. _____, officially the People's Republic of _____, is a sovereign state located in East Asia. It is the world's most populous country, with a population of over 1.35 billion. The PRC is a single-party state governed by the Communist Party, with its seat of government in the capital city of Beijing.

   a. Central Asian-American Enterprise Fund
   b. Sino-Soviet split
   c. Fuel protests in the United Kingdom
   d. China

4. _____ is insurance against the risk of incurring medical expenses among individuals. By estimating the overall risk of health care and health system expenses, among a targeted group, an insurer can develop a routine finance structure, such as a monthly premium or payroll tax, to ensure that money is available to pay for the health care benefits specified in the insurance agreement. The benefit is administered by a central organization such as a government agency, private business, or not-for-profit entity.

   a. Health insurance
   b. Capitation
   c. Case mix group
   d. Centre for Reviews and Dissemination

5. _____ in general, describes the extent to which time, effort or cost is well used for the intended task or purpose. It is often used with the specific purpose of relaying the capability of a specific application of effort to produce a specific outcome effectively with a minimum amount or quantity of waste, expense, or unnecessary effort. '_____' has widely varying meanings in different disciplines.

   a. Efficiency
   b. Benefit incidence
   c. Blanket order
   d. Bond

1. a

2. d

3. d

4. a

5. a

You can take the complete Online Interactive Chapter Practice Test

for 4. Socioeconomic disparities in health
on all key terms, persons, places, and concepts.

No Additional Costs

http://www.Cram101.com

Register, send an email request to Travis.Reese@Cram101.com to get your user Id and password.

Include your customer order number, and ISBN number from your studyguide Retailer.

CHAPTER OUTLINE: KEY TERMS, PEOPLE, PLACES, CONCEPTS

	Medicare
	Wage
	Net present value
	Present value
	Value
	CARE
	Demand
	Internal rate of return
	Returns
	Specialization
	Insurance
	Monopoly
	Committee
	Index
	Liability
	Liability insurance
	Price
	Price index

5. The labor market for physicians

Medicare	In the United States, Medicare is a national social insurance program, administered by the U.S. federal government since 1966, that guarantees access to health insurance for Americans aged 65 and older who have worked and paid into the system, and younger people with disabilities as well as people with end stage renal disease (Medicare.gov, 2012) and persons with amyotrophic lateral sclerosis. As a social insurance program, Medicare spreads the financial risk associated with illness across society to protect everyone, and thus has a somewhat different social role from for-profit private insurers, which manage their risk portfolio by adjusting their pricing according to perceived risk. In 2010, Medicare provided health insurance to 48 million Americans--40 million people age 65 and older and eight million younger people with disabilities.
Wage	A wage is monetary compensation paid by an employer to an employee in exchange for work done. Payment may be calculated as a fixed amount for each task completed (a task wage or piece rate), or at an hourly or daily rate, or based on an easily measured quantity of work done. Payment by wage contrasts with salaried work, in which the employer pays an arranged amount at steady intervals (such as a week or month) regardless of hours worked, with commission which conditions pay on individual performance, and with compensation based on the performance of the company as a whole.
Net present value	In finance, the net present value or net present worth (NPW) of a time series of cash flows, both incoming and outgoing, is defined as the sum of the present values (PVs) of the individual cash flows of the same entity. In the case when all future cash flows are incoming (such as coupons and principal of a bond) and the only outflow of cash is the purchase price, the Net present value is simply the PV of future cash flows minus the purchase price (which is its own PV). Net present value is a central tool in discounted cash flow (DCF) analysis and is a standard method for using the time value of money to appraise long-term projects.
Present value	Present value, also known as present discounted value, is a future amount of money that has been discounted to reflect its current value, as if it existed today. The present value is always less than or equal to the future value because money has interest-earning potential, a characteristic referred to as the time value of money. Time value can be described with the simplified phrase, "A dollar today is worth more than a dollar tomorrow".
Value	Economic value is a measure of the benefit that an economic actor can gain from either a good or service. It is generally measured relative to units of currency, and the interpretation is therefore 'what is the maximum amount of money a specific actor is willing and able to pay for the good or service'?

Note that economic value is not the same as market price. If a consumer is willing to buy a good, it implies that the customer places a higher value on the good than the market price.

CARE	CARE is a major international humanitarian agency delivering broad-spectrum emergency relief and long-term international development projects. Founded in 1945, CARE is nonsectarian, non-partisan, and non-governmental. It is one of the largest and oldest humanitarian aid organizations focused on fighting global poverty.
Demand	In economics, demand for a good or service is an entire listing of the quantity of the good or service that a market would choose to buy, for every possible market price of the good or service. (Note: This distinguishes 'demand' from 'quantity demanded', where demand is a listing or graphing of quantity demanded at each possible price. In contrast to demand, quantity demanded is the exact quantity demanded at a certain price.
Internal rate of return	The internal rate of return or economic rate of return (ERR) is a rate of return used in capital budgeting to measure and compare the profitability of investments. It is also called the discounted cash flow rate of return (DCFROR). In the context of savings and loans the IRR is also called the effective interest rate.
Returns	Returns, in economics and political economy, are the distributions or payments awarded to the various suppliers of the factors of production.
Specialization	Specialization is the separation of tasks within a system. In a multicellular creature, cells are specialized for functions such as bone construction or oxygen transport. In capitalist societies, individual workers specialize for functions such as building construction or gasoline transport.
Insurance	Insurance is the equitable transfer of the risk of a loss, from one entity to another in exchange for payment. It is a form of risk management primarily used to hedge against the risk of a contingent, uncertain loss. According to study texts of The Chartered Insurance Institute, there are the following categories of risk:•Financial risks which means that the risk must have financial measurement.•Pure risks which means that the risk must be real and not related to gambling•Particular risks which means that these risks are not widespread in their effect, for example such as earthquake risk for the region prone to it. It is commonly accepted that only financial, pure and particular risks are insurable.

5. The labor market for physicians

Monopoly	A monopoly (from Greek monos μ???? + polein p??e?? (to sell)) exists when a specific person or enterprise is the only supplier of a particular commodity (this contrasts with a monopsony which relates to a single entity's control of a market to purchase a good or service, and with oligopoly which consists of a few entities dominating an industry). Monopolies are thus characterized by a lack of economic competition to produce the good or service and a lack of viable substitute goods. The verb 'monopolize' refers to the process by which a company gains the ability to raise prices or exclude competitors.
Committee	A committee is a type of small deliberative assembly that is usually intended to remain subordinate to another, larger deliberative assembly--which when organized so that action on committee requires a vote by all its entitled members, is called the 'Committee of the Whole'. Committees often serve several different functions:•Governance: in organizations considered too large for all the members to participate in decisions affecting the organization as a whole, a committee is given the power to make decisions, spend money, or take actions. Some or all such powers may be limited or effectively unlimited.
Index	In economics and finance, an index is a statistical measure of changes in a representative group of individual data points. These data may be derived from any number of sources, including company performance, prices, productivity, and employment. Economic indices (index, plural) track economic health from different perspectives.
Liability	A liability can mean something that is a hindrance or puts an individual or group at a disadvantage, or something that someone is responsible for, or something that increases the chance of something occurring . Liability may also refer in specific fields to:•Legal liability, the legal bound obligation to pay debts•Public liability, part of the law of tort which focuses on civil wrongs.
Liability insurance	Liability insurance is a part of the general insurance system of risk financing to protect the purchaser from the risks of liabilities imposed by lawsuits and similar claims. It protects the insured in the event he or she is sued for claims that come within the coverage of the insurance policy. Originally, individuals or companies that faced a common peril, formed a group and created a self-help fund out of which to pay compensation should any member incur loss (in other words, a mutual insurance arrangement).
Price	In ordinary usage, price is the quantity of payment or compensation given by one party to another in return for goods or services. In modern economies, prices are generally expressed in units of some form of currency. (For commodities, they are expressed as currency per unit weight of the commodity, e.g. euros per kilogram).

5. The labor market for physicians

Price index	A price index is a normalized average of price relatives for a given class of goods or services in a given region, during a given interval of time. It is a statistic designed to help to compare how these price relatives, taken as a whole, differ between time periods or geographical locations.
	Price indexes have several potential uses.

1. A _____ can mean something that is a hindrance or puts an individual or group at a disadvantage, or something that someone is responsible for, or something that increases the chance of something occurring .

   _____ may also refer in specific fields to:•Legal _____, the legal bound obligation to pay debts•Public _____, part of the law of tort which focuses on civil wrongs.

   a. Chancel repair liability
   b. Liability
   c. Corporate liability
   d. Directors and officers liability insurance

2. The _____ or economic rate of return (ERR) is a rate of return used in capital budgeting to measure and compare the profitability of investments. It is also called the discounted cash flow rate of return (DCFROR). In the context of savings and loans the IRR is also called the effective interest rate.

   a. Internal rate of return
   b. Benchmark-driven investment strategy
   c. Bielard, Biehl and Kaiser five-way model
   d. Bond credit rating

3. In economics, _____ for a good or service is an entire listing of the quantity of the good or service that a market would choose to buy, for every possible market price of the good or service. (Note: This distinguishes '_____' from 'quantity demanded', where _____ is a listing or graphing of quantity demanded at each possible price. In contrast to _____, quantity demanded is the exact quantity demanded at a certain price.

   a. Budget set
   b. Complementary good
   c. Consumer service
   d. Demand

5. The labor market for physicians

4. _____, also known as present discounted value, is a future amount of money that has been discounted to reflect its current value, as if it existed today. The _____ is always less than or equal to the future value because money has interest-earning potential, a characteristic referred to as the time value of money. Time value can be described with the simplified phrase, "A dollar today is worth more than a dollar tomorrow".

    a. Balloon payment mortgage
    b. Buydown
    c. Collateral
    d. Present value

5. In the United States, _____ is a national social insurance program, administered by the U.S. federal government since 1966, that guarantees access to health insurance for Americans aged 65 and older who have worked and paid into the system, and younger people with disabilities as well as people with end stage renal disease (_____.gov, 2012) and persons with amyotrophic lateral sclerosis. As a social insurance program, _____ spreads the financial risk associated with illness across society to protect everyone, and thus has a somewhat different social role from for-profit private insurers, which manage their risk portfolio by adjusting their pricing according to perceived risk.

    In 2010, _____ provided health insurance to 48 million Americans--40 million people age 65 and older and eight million younger people with disabilities.

    a. Bituah Leumi
    b. Child protection
    c. Medicare
    d. Coupon-eligible converter box

ANSWER KEY
5. The labor market for physicians

1. b
2. a
3. d
4. d
5. c

You can take the complete Online Interactive Chapter Practice Test

for 5. The labor market for physicians
on all key terms, persons, places, and concepts.

No Additional Costs

http://www.Cram101.com

Register, send an email request to Travis.Reese@Cram101.com to get your user Id and password.

Include your customer order number, and ISBN number from your studyguide Retailer.

6. The hospital industry

CHAPTER OUTLINE: KEY TERMS, PEOPLE, PLACES, CONCEPTS

	CARE
	Orphan drug
	Tropical disease
	China
	Health insurance
	Insurance
	Fee-for-service
	Payment
	Payment system
	Price
	Service
	Index
	Price index
	Cuba
	Experience
	Oligopoly
	Product
	Theory
	Market
	Market concentration
	Competition

6. The hospital industry

CHAPTER OUTLINE: KEY TERMS, PEOPLE, PLACES, CONCEPTS

_____ Demand

_____ Prescription

_____ Arms race

_____ Hypothesis

_____ Quality

_____ Race

_____ Foundation

_____ Trust

_____ Public hospital

_____ Adverse selection

_____ Profit

_____ Chargemaster

_____ Medicare

_____ Cost-shifting

CARE	CARE is a major international humanitarian agency delivering broad-spectrum emergency relief and long-term international development projects. Founded in 1945, CARE is nonsectarian, non-partisan, and non-governmental. It is one of the largest and oldest humanitarian aid organizations focused on fighting global poverty.
Orphan drug	An orphan drug is a pharmaceutical agent that has been developed specifically to treat a rare medical condition, the condition itself being referred to as an orphan disease. In the US and EU it is easier to gain marketing approval for an orphan drug, and there may be other financial incentives, such as extended exclusivity periods, all intended to encourage the development of drugs which might otherwise lack a sufficient profit motive. The assignment of orphan status to a disease and to any drugs developed to treat it is a matter of public policy in many countries, and has resulted in medical breakthroughs that may not have otherwise been achieved due to the economics of drug research and development.
Tropical disease	Tropical diseases are diseases that are prevalent in or unique to tropical and subtropical regions. The diseases are less prevalent in temperate climates, due in part to the occurrence of a cold season, which controls the insect population by forcing hibernation. Insects such as mosquitoes and flies are by far the most common disease carrier, or vector.
China	China, officially the People's Republic of China, is a sovereign state located in East Asia. It is the world's most populous country, with a population of over 1.35 billion. The PRC is a single-party state governed by the Communist Party, with its seat of government in the capital city of Beijing.
Health insurance	Health insurance is insurance against the risk of incurring medical expenses among individuals. By estimating the overall risk of health care and health system expenses, among a targeted group, an insurer can develop a routine finance structure, such as a monthly premium or payroll tax, to ensure that money is available to pay for the health care benefits specified in the insurance agreement. The benefit is administered by a central organization such as a government agency, private business, or not-for-profit entity.
Insurance	Insurance is the equitable transfer of the risk of a loss, from one entity to another in exchange for payment. It is a form of risk management primarily used to hedge against the risk of a contingent, uncertain loss. According to study texts of The Chartered Insurance Institute, there are the following categories of risk:•Financial risks which means that the risk must have financial measurement.•Pure risks which means that the risk must be real and not related to gambling•Particular risks which means that these risks are not widespread in their effect, for example such as earthquake risk for the region prone to it. It is commonly accepted that only financial, pure and particular risks are insurable.

6. The hospital industry

Fee-for-service	Fee-for-service is a payment model where services are unbundled and paid for separately. In health care, it gives an incentive for physicians to provide more treatments because payment is dependent on the quantity of care, rather than quality of care. Similarly, when patients are shielded from paying (cost-sharing) by health insurance coverage, they are incentivized to welcome any medical service that might do some good.
Payment	A payment is the transfer of an item of value from one party to another in exchange for the provision of goods, services or both, or to fulfill a legal obligation.
	The simplest and oldest form of payment is barter, the exchange of one good or service for another. In the modern world, common means of payment by an individual include money, cheque, debit, credit, or bank transfer, and in trade such payments are frequently preceded by an invoice or result in a receipt.
Payment system	The payment system is an operational network - governed by laws, rules and standards - that links bank accounts and provides the functionality for monetary exchange using bank deposits. The payment system is the infrastructure (consisting of institutions, instruments, rules, procedures, standards, and technical means) established to effect the transfer of monetary value between parties discharging mutual obligations. Its technical efficiency determines the efficiency with which transaction money is used in the economy, and risk associated with its use.
Price	In ordinary usage, price is the quantity of payment or compensation given by one party to another in return for goods or services.
	In modern economies, prices are generally expressed in units of some form of currency. (For commodities, they are expressed as currency per unit weight of the commodity, e.g. euros per kilogram).
Service	In economics, a service is an intangible commodity. That is, services are an example of intangible economic goods.
	Service provision is often an economic activity where the buyer does not generally, except by exclusive contract, obtain exclusive ownership of the thing purchased.
Index	In economics and finance, an index is a statistical measure of changes in a representative group of individual data points. These data may be derived from any number of sources, including company performance, prices, productivity, and employment. Economic indices (index, plural) track economic health from different perspectives.
Price index	A price index is a normalized average of price relatives for a given class of goods or services in a given region, during a given interval of time. It is a statistic designed to help to compare how these price relatives, taken as a whole, differ between time periods or geographical locations.

6. The hospital industry

Cuba	Cuba, officially the Republic of Cuba is an island country in the Caribbean. The nation of Cuba comprises the main island of Cuba, the Isla de la Juventud, and several archipelagos. Havana is the capital of Cuba and its largest city.
Experience	Experience comprises knowledge of or skill of some thing or some event gained through involvement in or exposure to that thing or event. The history of the word experience aligns it closely with the concept of experiment. For example, the word experience could be used in a statement like: 'I have experience in fishing'.
Oligopoly	An oligopoly is a market form in which a market or industry is dominated by a small number of sellers . Oligopolies can result from various forms of collusion which reduce competition and lead to higher prices for consumers.
	With few sellers, each oligopolist is likely to be aware of the actions of the others.
Product	In marketing, a product is anything that can be offered to a market that might satisfy a want or need. In retailing, products are called merchandise. In manufacturing, products are bought as raw materials and sold as finished goods.
Theory	Theory is a group of ideas meant to explain a certain topic of science, such as a single or collection of fact, event(s), or phenomen(a)(on). Typically, a theory is developed through the use of contemplative and rational forms of abstract and generalized thinking. Furthermore, a theory is often based on general principles that are independent of the thing being explained.
Market	A market is one of the many varieties of systems, institutions, procedures, social relations and infrastructures whereby parties engage in exchange. While parties may exchange goods and services by barter, most markets rely on sellers offering their goods or services (including labor) in exchange for money from buyers. It can be said that a market is the process by which the prices of goods and services are established.
Market concentration	In economics, market concentration is a function of the number of firms and their respective shares of the total production in a market. Alternative terms are Industry concentration and Seller concentration.
	Market concentration is related to industrial concentration, which concerns the distribution of production within an industry, as opposed to a market.
Competition	In economics, competition is the rivalry among sellers trying to achieve such goals as increasing profits, market share, and sales volume by varying the elements of the marketing mix: price, product, distribution, and promotion.

6. The hospital industry

	Merriam-Webster defines competition in business as 'the effort of two or more parties acting independently to secure the business of a third party by offering the most favorable terms.' It was described by Adam Smith in The Wealth of Nations (1776) and later economists as allocating productive resources to their most highly-valued uses and encouraging efficiency. Smith and other classical economists before Cournot were referring to price and non-price rivalry among producers to sell their goods on best terms by bidding of buyers, not necessarily to a large number of sellers nor to a market in final equilibrium.
Demand	In economics, demand for a good or service is an entire listing of the quantity of the good or service that a market would choose to buy, for every possible market price of the good or service. (Note: This distinguishes 'demand' from 'quantity demanded', where demand is a listing or graphing of quantity demanded at each possible price. In contrast to demand, quantity demanded is the exact quantity demanded at a certain price.
Prescription	In law, prescription is the method of sovereignty transfer of a territory through international law analogous to the common law doctrine of adverse possession for private real-estate. Prescription involves the open encroachment by the new sovereign upon the territory in question for a prolonged period of time, acting as the sovereign, without protest or other contest by the original sovereign. This doctrine legalizes de jure the de facto transfer of sovereignty caused in part by the original sovereign's extended negligence and/or neglect of the area in question.
Arms race	The phrase arms race, in its original usage, is a competition between two or more parties to have the best armed forces. Each party competes to produce larger numbers of weapons, greater armies, or superior military technology in a technological escalation.
	International conflict specialist Theresa Clair Smith, defines the term as 'the participation of two or more nation-states in apparently competitive or interactive increases in quantity or quality of war material and/or persons under arms.'
	Nowadays the term is mostly used to describe any competition where there is no absolute goal, only the relative goal of staying ahead of the other competitors, essentially the goal of proving to be 'better'.
Hypothesis	A hypothesis is a proposed explanation for a phenomenon. For a hypothesis to be a scientific hypothesis, the scientific method requires that one can test it. Scientists generally base scientific hypotheses on previous observations that cannot satisfactorily be explained with the available scientific theories.
Quality	Quality in business, engineering and manufacturing has a pragmatic interpretation as the non-inferiority or superiority of something; it is also defined as fitness for purpose. Quality is a perceptual, conditional, and somewhat subjective attribute and may be understood differently by different people.

Race	Race is a classification system used to categorize humans into large and distinct populations or groups by anatomical, cultural, ethnic, genetic, geographical, historical, linguistic, religious, and/or social affiliation. First used to refer to speakers of a common language and then to denote national affiliations, in the 17th century, people began to use the term to relate to observable physical traits. Such use promoted hierarchies favorable to differing ethnic groups.
Foundation	Foundation is a skin coloured cosmetic applied to the face to create an even, uniform colour to the complexion, to cover flaws and, sometimes, to change the natural skintone. Foundation applied to the body is generally referred to as 'body painting.'
Trust	A 'trust,' or 'corporate trust' means a large business. Originally, it was Standard Oil, which was already the largest corporation in the world
Public hospital	A public hospital or government hospital is a hospital which is owned by a government and receives government funding. This type of hospital provides medical care free of charge, the cost of which is covered by the funding the hospital receives.
Adverse selection	Adverse selection, anti-selection, or negative selection is a term used in economics, insurance, risk management, and statistics. It refers to a market process in which undesired results occur when buyers and sellers have asymmetric information (access to different information); the 'bad' products or services are more likely to be selected. For example, a bank that sets one price for all of its checking account customers runs the risk of being adversely selected against by its low-balance, high-activity (and hence least profitable) customers.
Profit	In neoclassical microeconomic theory, the term profit has two related but distinct meanings. Economic profit is similar to accounting profit but smaller because it reflects the total opportunity costs (both explicit and implicit) of a venture to an investor. Normal profit refers to a situation in which the economic profit is zero.
Chargemaster	In the United States, the chargemaster, also known as charge master, or charge description master, is a comprehensive listing of items billable to a hospital patient or a patient's health insurance provider. In practice, it usually contains highly inflated prices at several times that of actual costs to the hospital. The chargemaster typically serves as the starting point for negotiations with patients and health insurance providers of what amount of money will actually be paid to the hospital.
Medicare	In the United States, Medicare is a national social insurance program, administered by the U.S. federal government since 1966, that guarantees access to health insurance for Americans aged 65 and older who have worked and paid into the system, and younger people with disabilities as well as people with end stage renal disease (Medicare.gov, 2012) and persons with amyotrophic lateral sclerosis.

6. The hospital industry

As a social insurance program, Medicare spreads the financial risk associated with illness across society to protect everyone, and thus has a somewhat different social role from for-profit private insurers, which manage their risk portfolio by adjusting their pricing according to perceived risk.

In 2010, Medicare provided health insurance to 48 million Americans--40 million people age 65 and older and eight million younger people with disabilities.

Cost-shifting

Cost-shifting is either an economic situation where one individual, group, or government underpays for a service, resulting another individual, group or government overpaying for a service . It can occur where one group pays a smaller share of costs than before, resulting in another group paying a larger share of costs than before (shifting compared to previous arrangement). Some commentators on health policy in the United States believe the former currently happens in Medicare and Medicaid as they underpay for services resulting in private insurers overpaying.

1. A _____ or government hospital is a hospital which is owned by a government and receives government funding. This type of hospital provides medical care free of charge, the cost of which is covered by the funding the hospital receives.

   a. Bituah Leumi
   b. Public hospital
   c. Children in Scotland
   d. Coupon-eligible converter box

2. _____ is insurance against the risk of incurring medical expenses among individuals. By estimating the overall risk of health care and health system expenses, among a targeted group, an insurer can develop a routine finance structure, such as a monthly premium or payroll tax, to ensure that money is available to pay for the health care benefits specified in the insurance agreement. The benefit is administered by a central organization such as a government agency, private business, or not-for-profit entity.

   a. Bundled payment
   b. Health insurance
   c. Case mix group
   d. Centre for Reviews and Dissemination

3. . An _____ is a pharmaceutical agent that has been developed specifically to treat a rare medical condition, the condition itself being referred to as an orphan disease.

In the US and EU it is easier to gain marketing approval for an _____, and there may be other financial incentives, such as extended exclusivity periods, all intended to encourage the development of drugs which might otherwise lack a sufficient profit motive. The assignment of orphan status to a disease and to any drugs developed to treat it is a matter of public policy in many countries, and has resulted in medical breakthroughs that may not have otherwise been achieved due to the economics of drug research and development.

a. Bundled payment
b. Orphan drug
c. Case mix group
d. Centre for Reviews and Dissemination

4. In economics, _____ for a good or service is an entire listing of the quantity of the good or service that a market would choose to buy, for every possible market price of the good or service. (Note: This distinguishes '_____' from 'quantity demanded', where _____ is a listing or graphing of quantity demanded at each possible price. In contrast to _____, quantity demanded is the exact quantity demanded at a certain price.

a. Budget set
b. Complementary good
c. Demand
d. Consumption

5. _____ is a group of ideas meant to explain a certain topic of science, such as a single or collection of fact, event(s), or phenomen(a)(on). Typically, a _____ is developed through the use of contemplative and rational forms of abstract and generalized thinking. Furthermore, a _____ is often based on general principles that are independent of the thing being explained.

a. Bayesian probability
b. Berlin Circle
c. Theory
d. Biological determinism

1. b
2. b
3. b
4. c
5. c

You can take the complete Online Interactive Chapter Practice Test

for 6. The hospital industry
on all key terms, persons, places, and concepts.

No Additional Costs

http://www.Cram101.com

Register, send an email request to Travis.Reese@Cram101.com to get your user Id and password.

Include your customer order number, and ISBN number from your studyguide Retailer.

7. Demand for insurance

	Income
	Marginal utility
	Utility
	Demand
	Insurance
	Value
	CARE

Income

Income is the consumption and savings opportunity gained by an entity within a specified timeframe, which is generally expressed in monetary terms. However, for households and individuals, 'income is the sum of all the wages, salaries, profits, interests payments, rents and other forms of earnings received... in a given period of time.'

In the field of public economics, the term may refer to the accumulation of both monetary and non-monetary consumption ability, with the former (monetary) being used as a proxy for total income.

Marginal utility

In economics, the marginal utility of a good or service is the gain from an increase or loss from a decrease in the consumption of that good or service. Economists sometimes speak of a law of diminishing marginal utility, meaning that the first unit of consumption of a good or service yields more utility than the second and subsequent units, with a continuing reduction for greater amounts. The marginal decision rule states that a good or service should be consumed at a quantity at which the marginal utility is equal to the marginal cost.

Utility

Utility, or usefulness, is the ability of something to satisfy needs or wants. Utility is an important concept in economics and game theory, because it represents satisfaction experienced by the consumer of a good. Not coincidentally, a good is something that satisfies human wants and provides utility, for example, to a consumer making a purchase.

7. Demand for insurance

Demand	In economics, demand for a good or service is an entire listing of the quantity of the good or service that a market would choose to buy, for every possible market price of the good or service. (Note: This distinguishes 'demand' from 'quantity demanded', where demand is a listing or graphing of quantity demanded at each possible price. In contrast to demand, quantity demanded is the exact quantity demanded at a certain price.
Insurance	Insurance is the equitable transfer of the risk of a loss, from one entity to another in exchange for payment. It is a form of risk management primarily used to hedge against the risk of a contingent, uncertain loss. According to study texts of The Chartered Insurance Institute, there are the following categories of risk:•Financial risks which means that the risk must have financial measurement.•Pure risks which means that the risk must be real and not related to gambling•Particular risks which means that these risks are not widespread in their effect, for example such as earthquake risk for the region prone to it. It is commonly accepted that only financial, pure and particular risks are insurable.
Value	Economic value is a measure of the benefit that an economic actor can gain from either a good or service. It is generally measured relative to units of currency, and the interpretation is therefore 'what is the maximum amount of money a specific actor is willing and able to pay for the good or service'? Note that economic value is not the same as market price. If a consumer is willing to buy a good, it implies that the customer places a higher value on the good than the market price.
CARE	CARE is a major international humanitarian agency delivering broad-spectrum emergency relief and long-term international development projects. Founded in 1945, CARE is nonsectarian, non-partisan, and non-governmental. It is one of the largest and oldest humanitarian aid organizations focused on fighting global poverty.

7. Demand for insurance

1. _____ is the consumption and savings opportunity gained by an entity within a specified timeframe, which is generally expressed in monetary terms. However, for households and individuals, '_____ is the sum of all the wages, salaries, profits, interests payments, rents and other forms of earnings received... in a given period of time.'

   In the field of public economics, the term may refer to the accumulation of both monetary and non-monetary consumption ability, with the former (monetary) being used as a proxy for total _____.

   a. Fuel protests in the United Kingdom
   b. Battle of Annaberg
   c. Freikorps Lichtschlag
   d. Income

2. In economics, _____ for a good or service is an entire listing of the quantity of the good or service that a market would choose to buy, for every possible market price of the good or service. (Note: This distinguishes '_____' from 'quantity demanded', where _____ is a listing or graphing of quantity demanded at each possible price. In contrast to _____, quantity demanded is the exact quantity demanded at a certain price.

   a. Demand
   b. Complementary good
   c. Consumer service
   d. Consumption

3. In economics, the _____ of a good or service is the gain from an increase or loss from a decrease in the consumption of that good or service. Economists sometimes speak of a law of diminishing _____, meaning that the first unit of consumption of a good or service yields more utility than the second and subsequent units, with a continuing reduction for greater amounts. The marginal decision rule states that a good or service should be consumed at a quantity at which the _____ is equal to the marginal cost.

   a. Baker cube
   b. Bereavement benefit
   c. Biological standard of living
   d. Marginal utility

4. _____, or usefulness, is the ability of something to satisfy needs or wants. _____ is an important concept in economics and game theory, because it represents satisfaction experienced by the consumer of a good. Not coincidentally, a good is something that satisfies human wants and provides _____, for example, to a consumer making a purchase.

   a. Fuel protests in the United Kingdom
   b. Battle of Annaberg
   c. Utility
   d. Freikorps Oberland

5. . _____ is the equitable transfer of the risk of a loss, from one entity to another in exchange for payment.

It is a form of risk management primarily used to hedge against the risk of a contingent, uncertain loss.

According to study texts of The Chartered _____ Institute, there are the following categories of risk:•Financial risks which means that the risk must have financial measurement.•Pure risks which means that the risk must be real and not related to gambling•Particular risks which means that these risks are not widespread in their effect, for example such as earthquake risk for the region prone to it.

It is commonly accepted that only financial, pure and particular risks are insurable.

a. Fuel protests in the United Kingdom
b. Battle of Annaberg
c. Freikorps Lichtschlag
d. Insurance

1. d

2. a

3. d

4. c

5. d

You can take the complete Online Interactive Chapter Practice Test

for 7. Demand for insurance
on all key terms, persons, places, and concepts.

No Additional Costs

http://www.Cram101.com

Register, send an email request to Travis.Reese@Cram101.com to get your user Id and password.

Include your customer order number, and ISBN number from your studyguide Retailer.

8. Adverse selection: Akerlof`s market for lemons

_____	Adverse selection
_____	Distribution
_____	Quality
_____	Utility
_____	Market
_____	Control
_____	Demand
_____	Prescription
_____	Price
_____	Price controls

Adverse selection	Adverse selection, anti-selection, or negative selection is a term used in economics, insurance, risk management, and statistics. It refers to a market process in which undesired results occur when buyers and sellers have asymmetric information (access to different information); the 'bad' products or services are more likely to be selected. For example, a bank that sets one price for all of its checking account customers runs the risk of being adversely selected against by its low-balance, high-activity (and hence least profitable) customers.
Distribution	Distribution in economics refers to the way total output, income, or wealth is distributed among individuals or among the factors of production . In general theory and the national income and product accounts, each unit of output corresponds to a unit of income. One use of national accounts is for classifying factor incomes and measuring their respective shares, as in National Income.
Quality	Quality in business, engineering and manufacturing has a pragmatic interpretation as the non-inferiority or superiority of something; it is also defined as fitness for purpose.

	Quality is a perceptual, conditional, and somewhat subjective attribute and may be understood differently by different people. Consumers may focus on the specification quality of a product/service, or how it compares to competitors in the marketplace.
Utility	Utility, or usefulness, is the ability of something to satisfy needs or wants. Utility is an important concept in economics and game theory, because it represents satisfaction experienced by the consumer of a good. Not coincidentally, a good is something that satisfies human wants and provides utility, for example, to a consumer making a purchase.
Market	A market is one of the many varieties of systems, institutions, procedures, social relations and infrastructures whereby parties engage in exchange. While parties may exchange goods and services by barter, most markets rely on sellers offering their goods or services (including labor) in exchange for money from buyers. It can be said that a market is the process by which the prices of goods and services are established.
Control	Controlling is one of the managerial functions like planning, organizing, staffing and directing. It is an important function because it helps to check the errors and to take the corrective action so that deviation from standards are minimized and stated goals of the organization are achieved in a desired manner. According to modern concepts, control is a foreseeing action whereas earlier concept of control was used only when errors were detected.
Demand	In economics, demand for a good or service is an entire listing of the quantity of the good or service that a market would choose to buy, for every possible market price of the good or service. (Note: This distinguishes 'demand' from 'quantity demanded', where demand is a listing or graphing of quantity demanded at each possible price. In contrast to demand, quantity demanded is the exact quantity demanded at a certain price.
Prescription	In law, prescription is the method of sovereignty transfer of a territory through international law analogous to the common law doctrine of adverse possession for private real-estate. Prescription involves the open encroachment by the new sovereign upon the territory in question for a prolonged period of time, acting as the sovereign, without protest or other contest by the original sovereign. This doctrine legalizes de jure the de facto transfer of sovereignty caused in part by the original sovereign's extended negligence and/or neglect of the area in question.
Price	In ordinary usage, price is the quantity of payment or compensation given by one party to another in return for goods or services. In modern economies, prices are generally expressed in units of some form of currency. (For commodities, they are expressed as currency per unit weight of the commodity, e.g.

8. Adverse selection: Akerlof's market for lemons

Price controls	Price controls are governmental restrictions on the prices that can be charged for goods and services in a market. The intent behind implementing such controls can stem from the desire to maintain affordability of staple foods and goods, to prevent price gouging during shortages, and to slow inflation, or, alternatively, to insure a minimum income for providers of certain goods or a minimum wage. There are two primary forms of price control, a price ceiling, the maximum price that can be charged, and a price floor, the minimum price that can be charged.

1. _____ in business, engineering and manufacturing has a pragmatic interpretation as the non-inferiority or superiority of something; it is also defined as fitness for purpose. _____ is a perceptual, conditional, and somewhat subjective attribute and may be understood differently by different people. Consumers may focus on the specification _____ of a product/service, or how it compares to competitors in the marketplace.

    a. 100 Best Workplaces in Europe
    b. Career portfolio
    c. CESG Claims Tested Mark
    d. Quality

2. _____, anti-selection, or negative selection is a term used in economics, insurance, risk management, and statistics. It refers to a market process in which undesired results occur when buyers and sellers have asymmetric information (access to different information); the 'bad' products or services are more likely to be selected. For example, a bank that sets one price for all of its checking account customers runs the risk of being adversely selected against by its low-balance, high-activity (and hence least profitable) customers.

    a. Adverse selection
    b. Battle of Annaberg
    c. Freikorps Lichtschlag
    d. Freikorps Oberland

3. . _____ in economics refers to the way total output, income, or wealth is distributed among individuals or among the factors of production . In general theory and the national income and product accounts, each unit of output corresponds to a unit of income. One use of national accounts is for classifying factor incomes and measuring their respective shares, as in National Income.

    a. Distribution
    b. Benefit incidence
    c. Blanket order

4. _____, or usefulness, is the ability of something to satisfy needs or wants. _____ is an important concept in economics and game theory, because it represents satisfaction experienced by the consumer of a good. Not coincidentally, a good is something that satisfies human wants and provides _____, for example, to a consumer making a purchase.

   a. Fuel protests in the United Kingdom
   b. Utility
   c. Freikorps Lichtschlag
   d. Freikorps Oberland

5. In law, _____ is the method of sovereignty transfer of a territory through international law analogous to the common law doctrine of adverse possession for private real-estate. _____ involves the open encroachment by the new sovereign upon the territory in question for a prolonged period of time, acting as the sovereign, without protest or other contest by the original sovereign. This doctrine legalizes de jure the de facto transfer of sovereignty caused in part by the original sovereign's extended negligence and/or neglect of the area in question.

   a. Bombardier Aerospace and Embraer S.A. government subsidy controversy
   b. Cabotage
   c. Prescription
   d. Central Authority

1. d

2. a

3. a

4. b

5. c

You can take the complete Online Interactive Chapter Practice Test

for 8. Adverse selection: Akerlof's market for lemons
on all key terms, persons, places, and concepts.

No Additional Costs

http://www.Cram101.com

Register, send an email request to Travis.Reese@Cram101.com to get your user Id and password.

Include your customer order number, and ISBN number from your studyguide Retailer.

9. Adverse selection: the Rothschild—Stiglitz model

	Health insurance
	Insurance
	Line
	Market
	Indifference curve
	Demand
	Committee

CHAPTER HIGHLIGHTS & NOTES: KEY TERMS, PEOPLE, PLACES, CONCEPTS

Health insurance	Health insurance is insurance against the risk of incurring medical expenses among individuals. By estimating the overall risk of health care and health system expenses, among a targeted group, an insurer can develop a routine finance structure, such as a monthly premium or payroll tax, to ensure that money is available to pay for the health care benefits specified in the insurance agreement. The benefit is administered by a central organization such as a government agency, private business, or not-for-profit entity.
Insurance	Insurance is the equitable transfer of the risk of a loss, from one entity to another in exchange for payment. It is a form of risk management primarily used to hedge against the risk of a contingent, uncertain loss. According to study texts of The Chartered Insurance Institute, there are the following categories of risk:•Financial risks which means that the risk must have financial measurement.•Pure risks which means that the risk must be real and not related to gambling•Particular risks which means that these risks are not widespread in their effect, for example such as earthquake risk for the region prone to it. It is commonly accepted that only financial, pure and particular risks are insurable.
Line	The lines of partition used to divide and vary fields and charges in heraldry are by default straight, but may have many different shapes.

Care must sometimes be taken to distinguish these types of lines from the extremely unusual and non-traditional use of lines as charges, and to distinguish these shapes from actual charges, such as 'a mount [or triple mount] in base,' or, particularly in German heraldry, different kinds of embattled from castle walls.

In Scotland, varied lines of partition are often used to modify a bordure (or sometimes another ordinary) to difference the arms of a cadet from the chief of the house.

Market

A market is one of the many varieties of systems, institutions, procedures, social relations and infrastructures whereby parties engage in exchange. While parties may exchange goods and services by barter, most markets rely on sellers offering their goods or services (including labor) in exchange for money from buyers. It can be said that a market is the process by which the prices of goods and services are established.

Indifference curve

In microeconomic theory, an indifference curve is a graph showing different bundles of goods between which a consumer is indifferent. That is, at each point on the curve, the consumer has no preference for one bundle over another. One can equivalently refer to each point on the indifference curve as rendering the same level of utility (satisfaction) for the consumer.

Demand

In economics, demand for a good or service is an entire listing of the quantity of the good or service that a market would choose to buy, for every possible market price of the good or service. (Note: This distinguishes 'demand' from 'quantity demanded', where demand is a listing or graphing of quantity demanded at each possible price. In contrast to demand, quantity demanded is the exact quantity demanded at a certain price.

Committee

A committee is a type of small deliberative assembly that is usually intended to remain subordinate to another, larger deliberative assembly--which when organized so that action on committee requires a vote by all its entitled members, is called the 'Committee of the Whole'. Committees often serve several different functions:•Governance: in organizations considered too large for all the members to participate in decisions affecting the organization as a whole, a committee is given the power to make decisions, spend money, or take actions. Some or all such powers may be limited or effectively unlimited.

9. Adverse selection: the Rothschild—Stiglitz model

1. _____ is insurance against the risk of incurring medical expenses among individuals. By estimating the overall risk of health care and health system expenses, among a targeted group, an insurer can develop a routine finance structure, such as a monthly premium or payroll tax, to ensure that money is available to pay for the health care benefits specified in the insurance agreement. The benefit is administered by a central organization such as a government agency, private business, or not-for-profit entity.

   a. Health insurance
   b. Capitation
   c. Case mix group
   d. Centre for Reviews and Dissemination

2. In microeconomic theory, an _____ is a graph showing different bundles of goods between which a consumer is indifferent. That is, at each point on the curve, the consumer has no preference for one bundle over another. One can equivalently refer to each point on the _____ as rendering the same level of utility (satisfaction) for the consumer.

   a. Indifference curve
   b. Bliss point
   c. Club good
   d. Conjectural variation

3. _____ is the equitable transfer of the risk of a loss, from one entity to another in exchange for payment. It is a form of risk management primarily used to hedge against the risk of a contingent, uncertain loss.

   According to study texts of The Chartered _____ Institute, there are the following categories of risk:•Financial risks which means that the risk must have financial measurement.•Pure risks which means that the risk must be real and not related to gambling•Particular risks which means that these risks are not widespread in their effect, for example such as earthquake risk for the region prone to it.

   It is commonly accepted that only financial, pure and particular risks are insurable.

   a. Insurance
   b. Battle of Annaberg
   c. Freikorps Lichtschlag
   d. Freikorps Oberland

4. . A _____ is one of the many varieties of systems, institutions, procedures, social relations and infrastructures whereby parties engage in exchange. While parties may exchange goods and services by barter, most _____s rely on sellers offering their goods or services (including labor) in exchange for money from buyers. It can be said that a _____ is the process by which the prices of goods and services are established.

   a. Financial market
   b. Market
   c. Battle of Annaberg

5. The _____s of partition used to divide and vary fields and charges in heraldry are by default straight, but may have many different shapes. Care must sometimes be taken to distinguish these types of _____s from the extremely unusual and non-traditional use of _____s as charges, and to distinguish these shapes from actual charges, such as 'a mount [or triple mount] in base,' or, particularly in German heraldry, different kinds of embattled from castle walls.

    In Scotland, varied _____s of partition are often used to modify a bordure (or sometimes another ordinary) to difference the arms of a cadet from the chief of the house.

    a. Banderole
    b. Baron and feme
    c. Blazon
    d. Line

1. a

2. a

3. a

4. b

5. d

You can take the complete Online Interactive Chapter Practice Test

for 9. Adverse selection: the Rothschild—Stiglitz model
on all key terms, persons, places, and concepts.

No Additional Costs

http://www.Cram101.com

Register, send an email request to Travis.Reese@Cram101.com to get your user Id and password.

Include your customer order number, and ISBN number from your studyguide Retailer.

10. Adverse selection in real markets

Health insurance

Insurance

Information asymmetry

Problem

Adverse selection

Market

Committee

Cuba

Retirement

Medicaid

Settlement

Viatical settlement

CARE

10. Adverse selection in real markets

Health insurance	Health insurance is insurance against the risk of incurring medical expenses among individuals. By estimating the overall risk of health care and health system expenses, among a targeted group, an insurer can develop a routine finance structure, such as a monthly premium or payroll tax, to ensure that money is available to pay for the health care benefits specified in the insurance agreement. The benefit is administered by a central organization such as a government agency, private business, or not-for-profit entity.
Insurance	Insurance is the equitable transfer of the risk of a loss, from one entity to another in exchange for payment. It is a form of risk management primarily used to hedge against the risk of a contingent, uncertain loss. According to study texts of The Chartered Insurance Institute, there are the following categories of risk:•Financial risks which means that the risk must have financial measurement.•Pure risks which means that the risk must be real and not related to gambling•Particular risks which means that these risks are not widespread in their effect, for example such as earthquake risk for the region prone to it. It is commonly accepted that only financial, pure and particular risks are insurable.
Information asymmetry	In contract theory and economics, information asymmetry deals with the study of decisions in transactions where one party has more or better information than the other. This creates an imbalance of power in transactions which can sometimes cause the transactions to go awry, a kind of market failure in the worst case. Examples of this problem are adverse selection, moral hazard, and information monopoly.
Problem	A problem, which can be caused for different reasons, and, if solvable, can usually be solved in a number of different ways, is defined in a number of different ways. This is determined by the context in which a said problems is defined. When discussed, a problem can be argued in multiple ways.
Adverse selection	Adverse selection, anti-selection, or negative selection is a term used in economics, insurance, risk management, and statistics. It refers to a market process in which undesired results occur when buyers and sellers have asymmetric information (access to different information); the 'bad' products or services are more likely to be selected. For example, a bank that sets one price for all of its checking account customers runs the risk of being adversely selected against by its low-balance, high-activity (and hence least profitable) customers.
Market	A market is one of the many varieties of systems, institutions, procedures, social relations and infrastructures whereby parties engage in exchange. While parties may exchange goods and services by barter, most markets rely on sellers offering their goods or services (including labor) in exchange for money from buyers.

10. Adverse selection in real markets

Committee	A committee is a type of small deliberative assembly that is usually intended to remain subordinate to another, larger deliberative assembly--which when organized so that action on committee requires a vote by all its entitled members, is called the 'Committee of the Whole'. Committees often serve several different functions:•Governance: in organizations considered too large for all the members to participate in decisions affecting the organization as a whole, a committee is given the power to make decisions, spend money, or take actions. Some or all such powers may be limited or effectively unlimited.
Cuba	Cuba, officially the Republic of Cuba is an island country in the Caribbean. The nation of Cuba comprises the main island of Cuba, the Isla de la Juventud, and several archipelagos. Havana is the capital of Cuba and its largest city.
Retirement	Retirement is the point where a person stops employment completely. A person may also semi-retire by reducing work hours. Many people choose to retire when they are eligible for private or public pension benefits, although some are forced to retire when physical conditions no longer allow the person to work any more (by illness or accident) or as a result of legislation concerning their position.
Medicaid	Medicaid in the United States is a social health care program for families and individuals with low income and resources. The Health Insurance Association of America describes Medicaid as a 'government insurance program for persons of all ages whose income and resources are insufficient to pay for health care.' (America's Health Insurance Plans (HIAA), pg. 232). Medicaid is the largest source of funding for medical and health-related services for people with low income in the United States.
Settlement	Settlement of securities is a business process whereby securities or interests in securities are delivered, usually against payment of money, to fulfill contractual obligations, such as those arising under securities trades. In the U.S., the settlement date for marketable stocks is usually 3 business days after the trade is executed, and for listed options and government securities it is usually 1 day after the execution. As part of performance on the delivery obligations entailed by the trade, settlement involves the delivery of securities and the corresponding payment.
Viatical settlement	A viatical settlement is the sale of a policy owner's existing life insurance policy to a third party for more than its cash surrender value, but less than its net death benefit. Such a sale provides the policy owner with an lump sum. The third party becomes the new owner of the policy, pays the monthly premiums, and receives the full benefit of the policy when the insured dies.

10. Adverse selection in real markets

CARE	CARE is a major international humanitarian agency delivering broad-spectrum emergency relief and long-term international development projects. Founded in 1945, CARE is nonsectarian, non-partisan, and non-governmental. It is one of the largest and oldest humanitarian aid organizations focused on fighting global poverty.

1. A _____ is the sale of a policy owner's existing life insurance policy to a third party for more than its cash surrender value, but less than its net death benefit. Such a sale provides the policy owner with an lump sum. The third party becomes the new owner of the policy, pays the monthly premiums, and receives the full benefit of the policy when the insured dies.

   a. Boiler insurance
   b. Viatical settlement
   c. Business owner%27s policy
   d. Catastrophe bond

2. _____ is a major international humanitarian agency delivering broad-spectrum emergency relief and long-term international development projects. Founded in 1945, _____ is nonsectarian, non-partisan, and non-governmental. It is one of the largest and oldest humanitarian aid organizations focused on fighting global poverty.

   a. Bah%C3%A1%27%C3%AD International Community
   b. Benevolent Organisation for Development, Health and Insight
   c. Bethlehem Association
   d. CARE

3. A _____ is one of the many varieties of systems, institutions, procedures, social relations and infrastructures whereby parties engage in exchange. While parties may exchange goods and services by barter, most _____s rely on sellers offering their goods or services (including labor) in exchange for money from buyers. It can be said that a _____ is the process by which the prices of goods and services are established.

   a. Financial market
   b. Fuel protests in the United Kingdom
   c. Market
   d. Freikorps Lichtschlag

4. . _____ is insurance against the risk of incurring medical expenses among individuals.

10. Adverse selection in real markets

By estimating the overall risk of health care and health system expenses, among a targeted group, an insurer can develop a routine finance structure, such as a monthly premium or payroll tax, to ensure that money is available to pay for the health care benefits specified in the insurance agreement. The benefit is administered by a central organization such as a government agency, private business, or not-for-profit entity.

a. Bundled payment
b. Capitation
c. Case mix group
d. Health insurance

5. _____ is the point where a person stops employment completely. A person may also semi-retire by reducing work hours.

Many people choose to retire when they are eligible for private or public pension benefits, although some are forced to retire when physical conditions no longer allow the person to work any more (by illness or accident) or as a result of legislation concerning their position.

a. Banishment room
b. Constructive dismissal
c. Dismissal
d. Retirement

1. b
2. d
3. c
4. d
5. d

You can take the complete Online Interactive Chapter Practice Test

for 10. Adverse selection in real markets
on all key terms, persons, places, and concepts.

No Additional Costs

http://www.Cram101.com

Register, send an email request to Travis.Reese@Cram101.com to get your user Id and password.

Include your customer order number, and ISBN number from your studyguide Retailer.

11. Moral hazard

CHAPTER OUTLINE: KEY TERMS, PEOPLE, PLACES, CONCEPTS

	Insurance
	Moral hazard
	Demand
	Distortion
	Prescription
	Price
	Budget
	Medicare
	Copayment
	Deductible
	Gatekeeping
	Health insurance
	Medicaid
	CARE
	Managed care
	Market
	Income

11. Moral hazard

Insurance	Insurance is the equitable transfer of the risk of a loss, from one entity to another in exchange for payment. It is a form of risk management primarily used to hedge against the risk of a contingent, uncertain loss. According to study texts of The Chartered Insurance Institute, there are the following categories of risk:•Financial risks which means that the risk must have financial measurement.•Pure risks which means that the risk must be real and not related to gambling•Particular risks which means that these risks are not widespread in their effect, for example such as earthquake risk for the region prone to it. It is commonly accepted that only financial, pure and particular risks are insurable.
Moral hazard	In economic theory, a moral hazard is a situation where a party will have a tendency to take risks because the costs that could result will not be felt by the party taking the risk. In other words, it is a tendency to be more willing to take a risk, knowing that the potential costs or burdens of taking such risk will be borne, in whole or in part, by others. A moral hazard may occur where the actions of one party may change to the detriment of another after a financial transaction has taken place.
Demand	In economics, demand for a good or service is an entire listing of the quantity of the good or service that a market would choose to buy, for every possible market price of the good or service. (Note: This distinguishes 'demand' from 'quantity demanded', where demand is a listing or graphing of quantity demanded at each possible price. In contrast to demand, quantity demanded is the exact quantity demanded at a certain price.
Distortion	A distortion is departure from the allocation of economic resources from the state in which each agent maximizes his/her own welfare. A proportional wage-income tax, for instance, is distortionary, whereas a lump-sum tax is not. In a competitive equilibrium, a proportional wage income tax discourages work.
Prescription	In law, prescription is the method of sovereignty transfer of a territory through international law analogous to the common law doctrine of adverse possession for private real-estate. Prescription involves the open encroachment by the new sovereign upon the territory in question for a prolonged period of time, acting as the sovereign, without protest or other contest by the original sovereign. This doctrine legalizes de jure the de facto transfer of sovereignty caused in part by the original sovereign's extended negligence and/or neglect of the area in question.
Price	In ordinary usage, price is the quantity of payment or compensation given by one party to another in return for goods or services. In modern economies, prices are generally expressed in units of some form of currency. (For commodities, they are expressed as currency per unit weight of the commodity, e.g.

Budget	A budget is a quantitative expression of a plan for a defined period of time. It may include planned sales volumes and revenues, resource quantities, costs and expenses, assets, liabilities and cash flows. It expresses strategic plans of business units, organizations, activities or events in measurable terms.
Medicare	In the United States, Medicare is a national social insurance program, administered by the U.S. federal government since 1966, that guarantees access to health insurance for Americans aged 65 and older who have worked and paid into the system, and younger people with disabilities as well as people with end stage renal disease (Medicare.gov, 2012) and persons with amyotrophic lateral sclerosis. As a social insurance program, Medicare spreads the financial risk associated with illness across society to protect everyone, and thus has a somewhat different social role from for-profit private insurers, which manage their risk portfolio by adjusting their pricing according to perceived risk. In 2010, Medicare provided health insurance to 48 million Americans--40 million people age 65 and older and eight million younger people with disabilities.
Copayment	In the United States, copayment or copay is a payment defined in the insurance policy and paid by the insured person each time a medical service is accessed. It is technically a form of coinsurance, but is defined differently in health insurance where a coinsurance is a percentage payment after the deductible up to a certain limit. It must be paid before any policy benefit is payable by an insurance company.
Deductible	In an insurance policy, the deductible is the amount of expenses that must be paid out of pocket before an insurer will pay any expenses. Example: if you have a $5000 deductible per year and you happen to spend $6000 this year, you will get your reimbursement for $1000 this year. In general usage, the term deductible may be used to describe one of several types of clauses that are used by insurance companies as a threshold for policy payments.
Gatekeeping	Gatekeeping is the process through which information is filtered for dissemination, whether for publication, broadcasting, the Internet, or some other mode of communication. The academic theory of gatekeeping is found in multiple fields of study, including communication studies, journalism, political science, and sociology. It was originally focused on the mass media with its few-to-many dynamic but now gatekeeping theory also addresses face-to-face communication and the many-to-many dynamic inherent in the Internet.
Health insurance	Health insurance is insurance against the risk of incurring medical expenses among individuals. By estimating the overall risk of health care and health system expenses, among a targeted group, an insurer can develop a routine finance structure, such as a monthly premium or payroll tax, to ensure that money is available to pay for the health care benefits specified in the insurance agreement.

11. Moral hazard

Medicaid	Medicaid in the United States is a social health care program for families and individuals with low income and resources. The Health Insurance Association of America describes Medicaid as a 'government insurance program for persons of all ages whose income and resources are insufficient to pay for health care.' (America's Health Insurance Plans (HIAA), pg. 232). Medicaid is the largest source of funding for medical and health-related services for people with low income in the United States.
CARE	CARE is a major international humanitarian agency delivering broad-spectrum emergency relief and long-term international development projects. Founded in 1945, CARE is nonsectarian, non-partisan, and non-governmental. It is one of the largest and oldest humanitarian aid organizations focused on fighting global poverty.
Managed care	The term managed care or managed health care is used in the United States to describe a variety of techniques intended to reduce the cost of providing health benefits and improve the quality of care ('managed care techniques'), for organizations that use those techniques or provide them as services to other organizations ('managed care organization' or 'MCO'), or to describe systems of financing and delivering health care to enrollees organized around managed care techniques and concepts ('managed care delivery systems'). ...intended to reduce unnecessary health care costs through a variety of mechanisms, including: economic incentives for physicians and patients to select less costly forms of care; programs for reviewing the medical necessity of specific services; increased beneficiary cost sharing; controls on inpatient admissions and lengths of stay; the establishment of cost-sharing incentives for outpatient surgery; selective contracting with health care providers; and the intensive management of high-cost health care cases. The programs may be provided in a variety of settings, such as Health Maintenance Organizations and Preferred Provider Organizations.
Market	A market is one of the many varieties of systems, institutions, procedures, social relations and infrastructures whereby parties engage in exchange. While parties may exchange goods and services by barter, most markets rely on sellers offering their goods or services (including labor) in exchange for money from buyers. It can be said that a market is the process by which the prices of goods and services are established.
Income	Income is the consumption and savings opportunity gained by an entity within a specified timeframe, which is generally expressed in monetary terms. However, for households and individuals, 'income is the sum of all the wages, salaries, profits, interests payments, rents and other forms of earnings received... in a given period of time.' In the field of public economics, the term may refer to the accumulation of both monetary and non-monetary consumption ability, with the former (monetary) being used as a proxy for total income.

11. Moral hazard

1. _____ is insurance against the risk of incurring medical expenses among individuals. By estimating the overall risk of health care and health system expenses, among a targeted group, an insurer can develop a routine finance structure, such as a monthly premium or payroll tax, to ensure that money is available to pay for the health care benefits specified in the insurance agreement. The benefit is administered by a central organization such as a government agency, private business, or not-for-profit entity.

   a. Bundled payment
   b. Capitation
   c. Case mix group
   d. Health insurance

2. A _____ is a quantitative expression of a plan for a defined period of time. It may include planned sales volumes and revenues, resource quantities, costs and expenses, assets, liabilities and cash flows. It expresses strategic plans of business units, organizations, activities or events in measurable terms.

   a. Rachel Ashwell
   b. Budget
   c. Battle of Annaberg
   d. Freikorps Lichtschlag

3. A _____ is departure from the allocation of economic resources from the state in which each agent maximizes his/her own welfare. A proportional wage-income tax, for instance, is distortionary, whereas a lump-sum tax is not. In a competitive equilibrium, a proportional wage income tax discourages work.

   a. Business cluster
   b. Distortion
   c. Fuel protests in the United Kingdom
   d. Battle of Annaberg

4. . The term _____ or managed health care is used in the United States to describe a variety of techniques intended to reduce the cost of providing health benefits and improve the quality of care ('_____ techniques'), for organizations that use those techniques or provide them as services to other organizations ('_____ organization' or 'MCO'), or to describe systems of financing and delivering health care to enrollees organized around _____ techniques and concepts ('_____ delivery systems'). '

   ...intended to reduce unnecessary health care costs through a variety of mechanisms, including: economic incentives for physicians and patients to select less costly forms of care; programs for reviewing the medical necessity of specific services; increased beneficiary cost sharing; controls on inpatient admissions and lengths of stay; the establishment of cost-sharing incentives for outpatient surgery; selective contracting with health care providers; and the intensive management of high-cost health care cases. The programs may be provided in a variety of settings, such as Health Maintenance Organizations and Preferred Provider Organizations.'

   a. Managed care

11. Moral hazard

b. Bottomry

c. Business owner%27s policy

d. Catastrophe bond

5. In the United States, _____ or copay is a payment defined in the insurance policy and paid by the insured person each time a medical service is accessed. It is technically a form of coinsurance, but is defined differently in health insurance where a coinsurance is a percentage payment after the deductible up to a certain limit. It must be paid before any policy benefit is payable by an insurance company.

a. Capitation

b. Copayment

c. Centre for Reviews and Dissemination

d. Chargemaster

---

1. d

2. b

3. b

4. a

5. b

You can take the complete Online Interactive Chapter Practice Test

for 11. Moral hazard
on all key terms, persons, places, and concepts.

No Additional Costs

http://www.Cram101.com

Register, send an email request to Travis.Reese@Cram101.com to get your user Id and password.

Include your customer order number, and ISBN number from your studyguide Retailer.

CHAPTER OUTLINE: KEY TERMS, PEOPLE, PLACES, CONCEPTS

	CARE
	Demand
	Pharmaceutical industry
	Induced innovation
	Innovation
	Patent
	Generic drug
	Consumer
	Black market
	Leakage
	Market
	Prescription
	Price
	Price discrimination
	Reimportation
	Control
	Price controls
	Health insurance
	Insurance
	Medicaid
	Orphan drug

12. Pharmaceuticals and the economics of innovation

	Tropical disease
	European Medicines Agency
	Access
	Advertising

CHAPTER HIGHLIGHTS & NOTES: KEY TERMS, PEOPLE, PLACES, CONCEPTS

CARE	CARE is a major international humanitarian agency delivering broad-spectrum emergency relief and long-term international development projects. Founded in 1945, CARE is nonsectarian, non-partisan, and non-governmental. It is one of the largest and oldest humanitarian aid organizations focused on fighting global poverty.
Demand	In economics, demand for a good or service is an entire listing of the quantity of the good or service that a market would choose to buy, for every possible market price of the good or service. (Note: This distinguishes 'demand' from 'quantity demanded', where demand is a listing or graphing of quantity demanded at each possible price. In contrast to demand, quantity demanded is the exact quantity demanded at a certain price.
Pharmaceutical industry	The pharmaceutical industry develops, produces, and markets drugs or pharmaceuticals licensed for use as medications. Pharmaceutical companies are allowed to deal in generic or brand medications and medical devices. They are subject to a variety of laws and regulations regarding the patenting, testing and ensuring safety and efficacy and marketing of drugs.
Induced innovation	Induced innovation is a macroeconomic hypothesis first proposed in 1932 by J.R. Hicks in his work The Theory of Wages. He proposed that 'a change in the relative prices of the factors of production is itself a spur to invention, and to invention of a particular kind--directed to economizing the use of a factor which has become relatively expensive.'
	Considerable literature has been produced on this hypothesis, which is often presented in terms of the effects of wage increases as an encouragement to labor-saving innovation. The hypothesis has also been applied to viewing increases in energy costs as a motivation for a more rapid improvement in energy efficiency of goods than would normally occur.

Innovation	Innovation is the application of better solutions that meet new requirements, in-articulated needs, or existing market needs. This is accomplished through more effective products, processes, services, technologies, or ideas that are readily available to markets, governments and society. The term innovation can be defined as something original and, as a consequence, new, that 'breaks into' the market or society.
Patent	A patent is a set of exclusive rights granted by a sovereign state to an inventor or assignee for a limited period of time in exchange for detailed public disclosure of an invention. An invention is a solution to a specific technological problem and is a product or a process. Patents are a form of intellectual property.
Generic drug	A generic drug is a drug defined as 'a drug product that is comparable to brand/reference listed drug product in dosage form, strength, route of administration, quality and performance characteristics, and intended use.' It has also been defined as a term referring to any drug marketed under its chemical name without advertising. Although they may not be associated with a particular company, generic drugs are subject to the regulations of the governments of countries where they are dispensed. Generic drugs are labeled with the name of the manufacturer and the adopted name (nonproprietary name) of the drug.
Consumer	A consumer is a person or group of people, such as a household, who are the final users of products or services. The consumer's use is final in the sense that the product is usually not improved by the use.
Black market	A black market or underground economy is the market in which goods or services are traded illegally. The key distinction of a black market trade is that the transaction itself is illegal. The goods or services may or may not themselves be illegal to own, or to trade through other, legal channels.
Leakage	In economics, a leakage is the non-consumption uses of income, including saving, taxes, and imports. In the Keynesian injection-leakage or circular flow model, leakages are combined with injections to identify equilibrium aggregate output. The model is best viewed as a circular flow between national income, output, consumption, and factor payments.
Market	A market is one of the many varieties of systems, institutions, procedures, social relations and infrastructures whereby parties engage in exchange. While parties may exchange goods and services by barter, most markets rely on sellers offering their goods or services (including labor) in exchange for money from buyers. It can be said that a market is the process by which the prices of goods and services are established.
Prescription	In law, prescription is the method of sovereignty transfer of a territory through international law analogous to the common law doctrine of adverse possession for private real-estate.

	Prescription involves the open encroachment by the new sovereign upon the territory in question for a prolonged period of time, acting as the sovereign, without protest or other contest by the original sovereign. This doctrine legalizes de jure the de facto transfer of sovereignty caused in part by the original sovereign's extended negligence and/or neglect of the area in question.
Price	In ordinary usage, price is the quantity of payment or compensation given by one party to another in return for goods or services.
	In modern economies, prices are generally expressed in units of some form of currency. (For commodities, they are expressed as currency per unit weight of the commodity, e.g. euros per kilogram).
Price discrimination	Price discrimination or price differentiation is a pricing strategy where identical or largely similar goods or services are transacted at different prices by the same provider in different markets or territories. Price differentiation is distinguished from product differentiation by the more substantial difference in production cost for the differently priced products involved in the latter strategy. Price differentiation essentially relies on the variation in the customers' willingness to pay.
Reimportation	Reimportation is the importation of goods into a country which had previously been exported from that country. A number of legal issues arise with the reimportation of goods, particularly where the goods were not designed for sale in the country from which they were initially exported. Because prices differ from one country to another, a reimporter may purchase goods in another country where they are sold at a low price and reimport them in order to undercut the price at which the goods are being sold in the country to which they are imported.
Control	Controlling is one of the managerial functions like planning, organizing, staffing and directing. It is an important function because it helps to check the errors and to take the corrective action so that deviation from standards are minimized and stated goals of the organization are achieved in a desired manner.
	According to modern concepts, control is a foreseeing action whereas earlier concept of control was used only when errors were detected.
Price controls	Price controls are governmental restrictions on the prices that can be charged for goods and services in a market. The intent behind implementing such controls can stem from the desire to maintain affordability of staple foods and goods, to prevent price gouging during shortages, and to slow inflation, or, alternatively, to insure a minimum income for providers of certain goods or a minimum wage. There are two primary forms of price control, a price ceiling, the maximum price that can be charged, and a price floor, the minimum price that can be charged.
Health insurance	Health insurance is insurance against the risk of incurring medical expenses among individuals.

	By estimating the overall risk of health care and health system expenses, among a targeted group, an insurer can develop a routine finance structure, such as a monthly premium or payroll tax, to ensure that money is available to pay for the health care benefits specified in the insurance agreement. The benefit is administered by a central organization such as a government agency, private business, or not-for-profit entity.
Insurance	Insurance is the equitable transfer of the risk of a loss, from one entity to another in exchange for payment. It is a form of risk management primarily used to hedge against the risk of a contingent, uncertain loss. According to study texts of The Chartered Insurance Institute, there are the following categories of risk:•Financial risks which means that the risk must have financial measurement.•Pure risks which means that the risk must be real and not related to gambling•Particular risks which means that these risks are not widespread in their effect, for example such as earthquake risk for the region prone to it. It is commonly accepted that only financial, pure and particular risks are insurable.
Medicaid	Medicaid in the United States is a social health care program for families and individuals with low income and resources. The Health Insurance Association of America describes Medicaid as a 'government insurance program for persons of all ages whose income and resources are insufficient to pay for health care.' (America's Health Insurance Plans (HIAA), pg. 232). Medicaid is the largest source of funding for medical and health-related services for people with low income in the United States.
Orphan drug	An orphan drug is a pharmaceutical agent that has been developed specifically to treat a rare medical condition, the condition itself being referred to as an orphan disease. In the US and EU it is easier to gain marketing approval for an orphan drug, and there may be other financial incentives, such as extended exclusivity periods, all intended to encourage the development of drugs which might otherwise lack a sufficient profit motive. The assignment of orphan status to a disease and to any drugs developed to treat it is a matter of public policy in many countries, and has resulted in medical breakthroughs that may not have otherwise been achieved due to the economics of drug research and development.
Tropical disease	Tropical diseases are diseases that are prevalent in or unique to tropical and subtropical regions. The diseases are less prevalent in temperate climates, due in part to the occurrence of a cold season, which controls the insect population by forcing hibernation. Insects such as mosquitoes and flies are by far the most common disease carrier, or vector.
European Medicines Agency	The European Medicines Agency is a European Union agency for the evaluation of medicinal products. From 1995 to 2004, the European Medicines Agency was known as European Agency for the Evaluation of Medicinal Products.

12. Pharmaceuticals and the economics of innovation

	Roughly parallel to the U.S. Food and Drug Administration (FDA), but without FDA-style centralisation, the European Medicines Agency was set up in 1995 with funding from the European Union and the pharmaceutical industry, as well as indirect subsidy from member states, in an attempt to harmonise (but not replace) the work of existing national medicine regulatory bodies.
Access	Access is a catalytic process that enables interactions, contact and exchanges among people, businesses and nations. An analytical framework to define the drivers and benefits of Access and to quantify the impact of Access on economic growth and personal well-being was created in 2006 by the Center for Science, Technology, and Economic Development at SRI International (formerly known as the Stanford Research Institute) in its study, "The Power of Access" (also titled, "How Greater Access Is Changing The World: A Landmark Study on the Relevance of Access to People, Businesses and Nations"). As outlined in the study, the Access framework consists of the Access Model, which expresses the function of Access as an econometric equation; the "Access Cycle"; and the 'Access Index,' which ranks 75 nations based on their performance in 22 metrics, including transportation infrastructure; telecommunications networks; trade policy; and news, media and information services.
Advertising	Advertising or advertizing in business is a form of marketing communication used to encourage, persuade, or manipulate an audience to take or continue to take some action. Most commonly, the desired result is to drive consumer behavior with respect to a commercial offering, although political and ideological advertising is also common. This type of work belongs to a category called affective labor.

1. A _____ is one of the many varieties of systems, institutions, procedures, social relations and infrastructures whereby parties engage in exchange. While parties may exchange goods and services by barter, most _____ s rely on sellers offering their goods or services (including labor) in exchange for money from buyers. It can be said that a _____ is the process by which the prices of goods and services are established.

   a. Financial market
   b. Fuel protests in the United Kingdom
   c. Battle of Annaberg
   d. Market

2. . _____ is a major international humanitarian agency delivering broad-spectrum emergency relief and long-term international development projects. Founded in 1945, _____ is nonsectarian, non-partisan, and non-governmental. It is one of the largest and oldest humanitarian aid organizations focused on fighting global poverty.

a. CARE

b. Benevolent Organisation for Development, Health and Insight

c. Bethlehem Association

d. Beyond Sport

3. _____ is a catalytic process that enables interactions, contact and exchanges among people, businesses and nations. An analytical framework to define the drivers and benefits of _____ and to quantify the impact of _____ on economic growth and personal well-being was created in 2006 by the Center for Science, Technology, and Economic Development at SRI International (formerly known as the Stanford Research Institute) in its study, "The Power of _____" (also titled, "How Greater _____ Is Changing The World: A Landmark Study on the Relevance of _____ to People, Businesses and Nations"). As outlined in the study, the _____ framework consists of the _____ Model, which expresses the function of _____ as an econometric equation; the "_____ Cycle"; and the '_____ Index,' which ranks 75 nations based on their performance in 22 metrics, including transportation infrastructure; telecommunications networks; trade policy; and news, media and information services.

a. Access

b. Economics

c. Economics handbooks

d. Spindletop

4. _____ or advertizing in business is a form of marketing communication used to encourage, persuade, or manipulate an audience to take or continue to take some action. Most commonly, the desired result is to drive consumer behavior with respect to a commercial offering, although political and ideological _____ is also common. This type of work belongs to a category called affective labor.

a. Finance

b. Advertising

c. Battle of Annaberg

d. Freikorps Lichtschlag

5. _____ in the United States is a social health care program for families and individuals with low income and resources. The Health Insurance Association of America describes _____ as a 'government insurance program for persons of all ages whose income and resources are insufficient to pay for health care.' (America's Health Insurance Plans (HIAA), pg. 232). _____ is the largest source of funding for medical and health-related services for people with low income in the United States.

a. Medicaid

b. Child Poverty Act 2010

c. Child Poverty Action Group

d. Compassion International

1. d
2. a
3. a
4. b
5. a

You can take the complete Online Interactive Chapter Practice Test

for 12. Pharmaceuticals and the economics of innovation
on all key terms, persons, places, and concepts.

No Additional Costs

http://www.Cram101.com

Register, send an email request to Travis.Reese@Cram101.com to get your user Id and password.

Include your customer order number, and ISBN number from your studyguide Retailer.

13. Technology and the price of health care

	CARE
	Consumer
	Index
	Price
	Price index
	Medicare
	Depression
	Atlas
	Production
	Production function
	Demand

CHAPTER HIGHLIGHTS & NOTES: KEY TERMS, PEOPLE, PLACES, CONCEPTS

CARE	CARE is a major international humanitarian agency delivering broad-spectrum emergency relief and long-term international development projects. Founded in 1945, CARE is nonsectarian, non-partisan, and non-governmental. It is one of the largest and oldest humanitarian aid organizations focused on fighting global poverty.
Consumer	A consumer is a person or group of people, such as a household, who are the final users of products or services. The consumer's use is final in the sense that the product is usually not improved by the use.
Index	In economics and finance, an index is a statistical measure of changes in a representative group of individual data points. These data may be derived from any number of sources, including company performance, prices, productivity, and employment.

13. Technology and the price of health care

Price	In ordinary usage, price is the quantity of payment or compensation given by one party to another in return for goods or services.
	In modern economies, prices are generally expressed in units of some form of currency. (For commodities, they are expressed as currency per unit weight of the commodity, e.g. euros per kilogram).
Price index	A price index is a normalized average of price relatives for a given class of goods or services in a given region, during a given interval of time. It is a statistic designed to help to compare how these price relatives, taken as a whole, differ between time periods or geographical locations.
	Price indexes have several potential uses.
Medicare	In the United States, Medicare is a national social insurance program, administered by the U.S. federal government since 1966, that guarantees access to health insurance for Americans aged 65 and older who have worked and paid into the system, and younger people with disabilities as well as people with end stage renal disease (Medicare.gov, 2012) and persons with amyotrophic lateral sclerosis. As a social insurance program, Medicare spreads the financial risk associated with illness across society to protect everyone, and thus has a somewhat different social role from for-profit private insurers, which manage their risk portfolio by adjusting their pricing according to perceived risk.
	In 2010, Medicare provided health insurance to 48 million Americans--40 million people age 65 and older and eight million younger people with disabilities.
Depression	In economics, a depression is a sustained, long-term downturn in economic activity in one or more economies. It is a more severe downturn than a recession, which is seen by some economists as inevitable part of capitalist economy.
	Considered by some economists to be a rare and extreme form of recession, a depression is characterized by its length; by abnormally large increases in unemployment; falls in the availability of credit, often due to some kind of banking or financial crisis; shrinking output as buyers dry up and suppliers cut back on production and investment; large number of bankruptcies including sovereign debt defaults; significantly reduced amounts of trade and commerce, especially international; as well as highly volatile relative currency value fluctuations, most often due to devaluations.
Atlas	In classical European architecture, an atlas is a support sculpted in the form of a man, which may take the place of a column, a pier or a pilaster. The Roman term for such a sculptural support is telamon (plural telamones or telamons).

13. Technology and the price of health care

Production	Production is a process of combining various material inputs and immaterial inputs in order to make something for consumption (the output). It is the act of creating output, a good or service which has value and contributes to the utility of individuals. Economic well-being is created in a production process, meaning all economic activities that aim directly or indirectly to satisfy human needs.
Production function	In economics, a production function relates physical output of a production process to physical inputs or factors of production. The production function is one of the key concepts of mainstream neoclassical theories, used to define marginal product and to distinguish allocative efficiency, the defining focus of economics. The primary purpose of the production function is to address allocative efficiency in the use of factor inputs in production and the resulting distribution of income to those factors, while abstracting away from the technological problems of achieving technical efficiency, as an engineer or professional manager might understand it.
Demand	In economics, demand for a good or service is an entire listing of the quantity of the good or service that a market would choose to buy, for every possible market price of the good or service. (Note: This distinguishes 'demand' from 'quantity demanded', where demand is a listing or graphing of quantity demanded at each possible price. In contrast to demand, quantity demanded is the exact quantity demanded at a certain price.

1. _____ is a process of combining various material inputs and immaterial inputs in order to make something for consumption (the output). It is the act of creating output, a good or service which has value and contributes to the utility of individuals. Economic well-being is created in a _____ process, meaning all economic activities that aim directly or indirectly to satisfy human needs.

   a. Capacity utilization
   b. Constant elasticity of transformation
   c. Production
   d. Diseconomies of scale

2. . _____ is a major international humanitarian agency delivering broad-spectrum emergency relief and long-term international development projects. Founded in 1945, _____ is nonsectarian, non-partisan, and non-governmental. It is one of the largest and oldest humanitarian aid organizations focused on fighting global poverty.

   a. Bah%C3%A1%27%C3%AD International Community
   b. Benevolent Organisation for Development, Health and Insight
   c. CARE

3. A _____ is a person or group of people, such as a household, who are the final users of products or services. The _____'s use is final in the sense that the product is usually not improved by the use.

   a. Base period
   b. Benefit incidence
   c. Consumer
   d. Bond

4. A _____ is a normalized average of price relatives for a given class of goods or services in a given region, during a given interval of time. It is a statistic designed to help to compare how these price relatives, taken as a whole, differ between time periods or geographical locations.

   Price indexes have several potential uses.

   a. Fuel protests in the United Kingdom
   b. Battle of Annaberg
   c. Price index
   d. Freikorps Oberland

5. In economics, _____ for a good or service is an entire listing of the quantity of the good or service that a market would choose to buy, for every possible market price of the good or service. (Note: This distinguishes '_____' from 'quantity demanded', where _____ is a listing or graphing of quantity demanded at each possible price. In contrast to _____, quantity demanded is the exact quantity demanded at a certain price.

   a. Budget set
   b. Demand
   c. Consumer service
   d. Consumption

1. c
2. c
3. c
4. c
5. b

You can take the complete Online Interactive Chapter Practice Test

for 13. Technology and the price of health care
on all key terms, persons, places, and concepts.

No Additional Costs

http://www.Cram101.com

Register, send an email request to Travis.Reese@Cram101.com to get your user Id and password.

Include your customer order number, and ISBN number from your studyguide Retailer.

14. Health technology assessment

	Retirement
	Health technology assessment
	Technology assessment
	Budget
	Cost-effectiveness analysis
	Medicaid
	Screening
	Cuba
	Medicare
	Utility
	Effectiveness
	Quality-adjusted life year
	Disability-adjusted life year
	Price
	Quality
	Quality of life
	Delphi
	Health insurance
	Insurance
	Rationing
	Value

	Equity
	Wealth

Retirement	Retirement is the point where a person stops employment completely. A person may also semi-retire by reducing work hours.
	Many people choose to retire when they are eligible for private or public pension benefits, although some are forced to retire when physical conditions no longer allow the person to work any more (by illness or accident) or as a result of legislation concerning their position.
Health technology assessment	Health technology assessment is a multi-disciplinary field of policy analysis that studies the medical, social, ethical, and economic implications of development, diffusion, and use of health technology. It has other definitions including 'the systematic evaluation of the properties and effects of a health technology, addressing the direct and intended effects of this technology, as well as its indirect and unintended consequences, and aimed mainly at informing decision making regarding health technologies.' and 'a multidisciplinary process that summarises information about the medical, social, economic and ethical issues related to the use of a health technology in a systematic, transparent, unbiased, robust manner. Its aim is to inform the formulation of safe, effective, health policies that are patient focused and seek to achieve best value.
Technology assessment	Technology assessment is a scientific, interactive, and communicative process that aims to contribute to the formation of public and political opinion on societal aspects of science and technology.
Budget	A budget is a quantitative expression of a plan for a defined period of time. It may include planned sales volumes and revenues, resource quantities, costs and expenses, assets, liabilities and cash flows. It expresses strategic plans of business units, organizations, activities or events in measurable terms.
Cost-effectiveness analysis	Cost-effectiveness analysis is a form of economic analysis that compares the relative costs and outcomes (effects) of two or more courses of action. Cost-effectiveness analysis is distinct from cost-benefit analysis, which assigns a monetary value to the measure of effect.

14. Health technology assessment

Medicaid	Medicaid in the United States is a social health care program for families and individuals with low income and resources. The Health Insurance Association of America describes Medicaid as a 'government insurance program for persons of all ages whose income and resources are insufficient to pay for health care.' (America's Health Insurance Plans (HIAA), pg. 232). Medicaid is the largest source of funding for medical and health-related services for people with low income in the United States.
Screening	Screening in economics refers to a strategy of combating adverse selection, one of the potential decision-making complications in cases of asymmetric information. The concept of screening was first developed by Michael Spence (1973), and should be distinguished from signalling, which implies that the informed agent moves first.
	For purposes of screening, asymmetric information cases assume two economic agents--which we call, for example, Abel and Cain--where Abel knows more about himself than Cain knows about Abel.
Cuba	Cuba, officially the Republic of Cuba is an island country in the Caribbean. The nation of Cuba comprises the main island of Cuba, the Isla de la Juventud, and several archipelagos. Havana is the capital of Cuba and its largest city.
Medicare	In the United States, Medicare is a national social insurance program, administered by the U.S. federal government since 1966, that guarantees access to health insurance for Americans aged 65 and older who have worked and paid into the system, and younger people with disabilities as well as people with end stage renal disease (Medicare.gov, 2012) and persons with amyotrophic lateral sclerosis. As a social insurance program, Medicare spreads the financial risk associated with illness across society to protect everyone, and thus has a somewhat different social role from for-profit private insurers, which manage their risk portfolio by adjusting their pricing according to perceived risk.
	In 2010, Medicare provided health insurance to 48 million Americans--40 million people age 65 and older and eight million younger people with disabilities.
Utility	Utility, or usefulness, is the ability of something to satisfy needs or wants. Utility is an important concept in economics and game theory, because it represents satisfaction experienced by the consumer of a good. Not coincidentally, a good is something that satisfies human wants and provides utility, for example, to a consumer making a purchase.
Effectiveness	Effectiveness is the capability of producing a desired result. When something is deemed effective, it means it has an intended or expected outcome, or produces a deep, vivid impression.
Quality-adjusted life year	The quality-adjusted life year or quality-adjusted life-year is a measure of disease burden, including both the quality and the quantity of life lived.

	It is used in assessing the value for money of a medical intervention. According to Pliskin et al., The Quality adjusted life year model requires utility independent, risk neutral, and constant proportional tradeoff behaviour.
Disability-adjusted life year	The disability-adjusted life year is a measure of overall disease burden, expressed as the number of years lost due to ill-health, disability or early death. Originally developed by Harvard University for the World Bank in 1990, the World Health Organization subsequently adopted the method in 1996 as part of the Ad hoc Committee on Health Research 'Investing in Health Research & Development' report. The Disability adjusted life year is becoming increasingly common in the field of public health and health impact assessment (HIA).
Price	In ordinary usage, price is the quantity of payment or compensation given by one party to another in return for goods or services. In modern economies, prices are generally expressed in units of some form of currency. (For commodities, they are expressed as currency per unit weight of the commodity, e.g. euros per kilogram).
Quality	Quality in business, engineering and manufacturing has a pragmatic interpretation as the non-inferiority or superiority of something; it is also defined as fitness for purpose. Quality is a perceptual, conditional, and somewhat subjective attribute and may be understood differently by different people. Consumers may focus on the specification quality of a product/service, or how it compares to competitors in the marketplace.
Quality of life	Quality of life is an important concern in economics, philosophy, political science, sociology and other fields. Quality of Life may also refer to:•Quality of life, a measure of the overall effect of medical issues on a patient•Quality of Life a 2004 drama starring Lane Garrison•'The Quality of Life' (Star Trek: The Next Generation), a TV episode•'The Quality of Life' (Yes Minister), a TV episode•'Quality of Life', an episode of The Dead Zone•The Quality of Life a 2008 TV movie following the series Da Vinci's Inquest and Da Vinci's City Hall.
Delphi	Delphi Forums is a former U.S. online service provider and since the mid 1990s has been a community internet forum site. It started as a nationwide dialup service in 1983. Delphi Forums remains active as of 2013, claiming 4 million registered members and 'more than 8,000 active Forums'.
Health insurance	Health insurance is insurance against the risk of incurring medical expenses among individuals.

14. Health technology assessment

By estimating the overall risk of health care and health system expenses, among a targeted group, an insurer can develop a routine finance structure, such as a monthly premium or payroll tax, to ensure that money is available to pay for the health care benefits specified in the insurance agreement. The benefit is administered by a central organization such as a government agency, private business, or not-for-profit entity.

Insurance	Insurance is the equitable transfer of the risk of a loss, from one entity to another in exchange for payment. It is a form of risk management primarily used to hedge against the risk of a contingent, uncertain loss.
	According to study texts of The Chartered Insurance Institute, there are the following categories of risk:•Financial risks which means that the risk must have financial measurement.•Pure risks which means that the risk must be real and not related to gambling•Particular risks which means that these risks are not widespread in their effect, for example such as earthquake risk for the region prone to it.
	It is commonly accepted that only financial, pure and particular risks are insurable.
Rationing	Rationing is the controlled distribution of scarce resources, goods, or services. Rationing controls the size of the ration, one's allotted portion of the resources being distributed on a particular day or at a particular time.
Value	Economic value is a measure of the benefit that an economic actor can gain from either a good or service. It is generally measured relative to units of currency, and the interpretation is therefore 'what is the maximum amount of money a specific actor is willing and able to pay for the good or service'?
	Note that economic value is not the same as market price. If a consumer is willing to buy a good, it implies that the customer places a higher value on the good than the market price.
Equity	In accounting and finance, equity is the residual claimant or interest of the most junior class of investors in assets, after all liabilities are paid; if liability exceeds assets, negative equity exists. In an accounting context, shareholders' equity represents the remaining interest in the assets of a company, spread among individual shareholders of common or preferred stock; a negative shareholders' equity is often referred to as a positive shareholders' deficit.
	At the very start of a business, owners put some funding into the business to finance operations.
Wealth	The modern understanding of Wealth is the abundance of valuable resources or material possessions. This excludes the core meaning as held in the originating old English word weal, which is from an Indo-European word stem.

1. _____ is the point where a person stops employment completely. A person may also semi-retire by reducing work hours.

   Many people choose to retire when they are eligible for private or public pension benefits, although some are forced to retire when physical conditions no longer allow the person to work any more (by illness or accident) or as a result of legislation concerning their position.

   a. Banishment room
   b. Constructive dismissal
   c. Dismissal
   d. Retirement

2. _____ is a multi-disciplinary field of policy analysis that studies the medical, social, ethical, and economic implications of development, diffusion, and use of health technology. It has other definitions including 'the systematic evaluation of the properties and effects of a health technology, addressing the direct and intended effects of this technology, as well as its indirect and unintended consequences, and aimed mainly at informing decision making regarding health technologies.' and 'a multidisciplinary process that summarises information about the medical, social, economic and ethical issues related to the use of a health technology in a systematic, transparent, unbiased, robust manner. Its aim is to inform the formulation of safe, effective, health policies that are patient focused and seek to achieve best value.

   a. Health technology assessment
   b. Career portfolio
   c. CESG Claims Tested Mark
   d. Commercial Product Assurance

3. _____ is a scientific, interactive, and communicative process that aims to contribute to the formation of public and political opinion on societal aspects of science and technology.

   a. 100 Best Workplaces in Europe
   b. Career portfolio
   c. CESG Claims Tested Mark
   d. Technology assessment

4. The _____ or quality-adjusted life-year is a measure of disease burden, including both the quality and the quantity of life lived. It is used in assessing the value for money of a medical intervention. According to Pliskin et al., The Quality adjusted life year model requires utility independent, risk neutral, and constant proportional tradeoff behaviour.

   a. Bundled payment
   b. Capitation
   c. Case mix group
   d. Quality-adjusted life year

5. . In the United States, _____ is a national social insurance program, administered by the U.S.

federal government since 1966, that guarantees access to health insurance for Americans aged 65 and older who have worked and paid into the system, and younger people with disabilities as well as people with end stage renal disease (_____.gov, 2012) and persons with amyotrophic lateral sclerosis. As a social insurance program, _____ spreads the financial risk associated with illness across society to protect everyone, and thus has a somewhat different social role from for-profit private insurers, which manage their risk portfolio by adjusting their pricing according to perceived risk.

In 2010, _____ provided health insurance to 48 million Americans--40 million people age 65 and older and eight million younger people with disabilities.

a. Bituah Leumi
b. Medicare
c. Children in Scotland
d. Coupon-eligible converter box

1. d
2. a
3. d
4. d
5. b

15. The health policy conundrum

CHAPTER OUTLINE: KEY TERMS, PEOPLE, PLACES, CONCEPTS

Equity

Wealth

Health insurance

Insurance

Adverse selection

Market

Option

Demand

Screening

Moral hazard

Budget

Cost-effectiveness analysis

Medicare

Copayment

Cost sharing

Gatekeeping

Sharing

Fee-for-service

Payment

Foundation

Trust

CARE

Health care

Need

Law

Price

Rationing

Control

Index

Prescription

Price controls

Price index

Economy

Production

Preference

Health equity

15. The health policy conundrum

Equity	In accounting and finance, equity is the residual claimant or interest of the most junior class of investors in assets, after all liabilities are paid; if liability exceeds assets, negative equity exists. In an accounting context, shareholders' equity represents the remaining interest in the assets of a company, spread among individual shareholders of common or preferred stock; a negative shareholders' equity is often referred to as a positive shareholders' deficit. At the very start of a business, owners put some funding into the business to finance operations.
Wealth	The modern understanding of Wealth is the abundance of valuable resources or material possessions. This excludes the core meaning as held in the originating old English word weal, which is from an Indo-European word stem. In this larger understanding of wealth, an individual, community, region or country that possesses an abundance of such possessions or resources to the benefit of the common good is known as wealthy.
Health insurance	Health insurance is insurance against the risk of incurring medical expenses among individuals. By estimating the overall risk of health care and health system expenses, among a targeted group, an insurer can develop a routine finance structure, such as a monthly premium or payroll tax, to ensure that money is available to pay for the health care benefits specified in the insurance agreement. The benefit is administered by a central organization such as a government agency, private business, or not-for-profit entity.
Insurance	Insurance is the equitable transfer of the risk of a loss, from one entity to another in exchange for payment. It is a form of risk management primarily used to hedge against the risk of a contingent, uncertain loss. According to study texts of The Chartered Insurance Institute, there are the following categories of risk:•Financial risks which means that the risk must have financial measurement.•Pure risks which means that the risk must be real and not related to gambling•Particular risks which means that these risks are not widespread in their effect, for example such as earthquake risk for the region prone to it. It is commonly accepted that only financial, pure and particular risks are insurable.
Adverse selection	Adverse selection, anti-selection, or negative selection is a term used in economics, insurance, risk management, and statistics. It refers to a market process in which undesired results occur when buyers and sellers have asymmetric information (access to different information); the 'bad' products or services are more likely to be selected. For example, a bank that sets one price for all of its checking account customers runs the risk of being adversely selected against by its low-balance, high-activity (and hence least profitable) customers.
Market	A market is one of the many varieties of systems, institutions, procedures, social relations and infrastructures whereby parties engage in exchange.

15. The health policy conundrum

	While parties may exchange goods and services by barter, most markets rely on sellers offering their goods or services (including labor) in exchange for money from buyers. It can be said that a market is the process by which the prices of goods and services are established.
Option	In finance, an option is a contract which gives the buyer the right, but not the obligation, to buy or sell an underlying asset or instrument at a specified strike price on or before a specified date. The seller has the corresponding obligation to fulfill the transaction - that is to sell or buy - if the buyer (owner) 'exercises' the option. The buyer pays a premium to the seller for this right.
Demand	In economics, demand for a good or service is an entire listing of the quantity of the good or service that a market would choose to buy, for every possible market price of the good or service. (Note: This distinguishes 'demand' from 'quantity demanded', where demand is a listing or graphing of quantity demanded at each possible price. In contrast to demand, quantity demanded is the exact quantity demanded at a certain price.
Screening	Screening in economics refers to a strategy of combating adverse selection, one of the potential decision-making complications in cases of asymmetric information. The concept of screening was first developed by Michael Spence (1973), and should be distinguished from signalling, which implies that the informed agent moves first. For purposes of screening, asymmetric information cases assume two economic agents--which we call, for example, Abel and Cain--where Abel knows more about himself than Cain knows about Abel.
Moral hazard	In economic theory, a moral hazard is a situation where a party will have a tendency to take risks because the costs that could result will not be felt by the party taking the risk. In other words, it is a tendency to be more willing to take a risk, knowing that the potential costs or burdens of taking such risk will be borne, in whole or in part, by others. A moral hazard may occur where the actions of one party may change to the detriment of another after a financial transaction has taken place.
Budget	A budget is a quantitative expression of a plan for a defined period of time. It may include planned sales volumes and revenues, resource quantities, costs and expenses, assets, liabilities and cash flows. It expresses strategic plans of business units, organizations, activities or events in measurable terms.
Cost-effectiveness analysis	Cost-effectiveness analysis is a form of economic analysis that compares the relative costs and outcomes (effects) of two or more courses of action. Cost-effectiveness analysis is distinct from cost-benefit analysis, which assigns a monetary value to the measure of effect. Cost-effectiveness analysis is often used in the field of health services, where it may be inappropriate to monetize health effect.
Medicare	In the United States, Medicare is a national social insurance program, administered by the U.S.

federal government since 1966, that guarantees access to health insurance for Americans aged 65 and older who have worked and paid into the system, and younger people with disabilities as well as people with end stage renal disease (Medicare.gov, 2012) and persons with amyotrophic lateral sclerosis. As a social insurance program, Medicare spreads the financial risk associated with illness across society to protect everyone, and thus has a somewhat different social role from for-profit private insurers, which manage their risk portfolio by adjusting their pricing according to perceived risk.

In 2010, Medicare provided health insurance to 48 million Americans--40 million people age 65 and older and eight million younger people with disabilities.

Copayment	In the United States, copayment or copay is a payment defined in the insurance policy and paid by the insured person each time a medical service is accessed. It is technically a form of coinsurance, but is defined differently in health insurance where a coinsurance is a percentage payment after the deductible up to a certain limit. It must be paid before any policy benefit is payable by an insurance company.
Cost sharing	In health care, cost sharing occurs when patients pay for a portion of health care costs not covered by health insurance. The 'out-of-pocket' payment varies among healthcare plans, and also depends on whether or not the patient chooses to use a healthcare provider who is contracted with the healthcare plan's network. Examples of out-of-pocket payments involved in cost sharing include copays, deductibles and coinsurance.
Gatekeeping	Gatekeeping is the process through which information is filtered for dissemination, whether for publication, broadcasting, the Internet, or some other mode of communication. The academic theory of gatekeeping is found in multiple fields of study, including communication studies, journalism, political science, and sociology. It was originally focused on the mass media with its few-to-many dynamic but now gatekeeping theory also addresses face-to-face communication and the many-to-many dynamic inherent in the Internet.
Sharing	Sharing is the joint use of a resource or space. In its narrow sense, it refers to joint or alternating use of an inherently finite good, such as a common pasture or a shared residence. It is also the process of dividing and distributing.
Fee-for-service	Fee-for-service is a payment model where services are unbundled and paid for separately. In health care, it gives an incentive for physicians to provide more treatments because payment is dependent on the quantity of care, rather than quality of care. Similarly, when patients are shielded from paying (cost-sharing) by health insurance coverage, they are incentivized to welcome any medical service that might do some good.
Payment	A payment is the transfer of an item of value from one party to another in exchange for the provision of goods, services or both, or to fulfill a legal obligation.

15. The health policy conundrum

	The simplest and oldest form of payment is barter, the exchange of one good or service for another. In the modern world, common means of payment by an individual include money, cheque, debit, credit, or bank transfer, and in trade such payments are frequently preceded by an invoice or result in a receipt.
Foundation	Foundation is a skin coloured cosmetic applied to the face to create an even, uniform colour to the complexion, to cover flaws and, sometimes, to change the natural skintone. Foundation applied to the body is generally referred to as 'body painting.'
Trust	A 'trust,' or 'corporate trust' means a large business. Originally, it was Standard Oil, which was already the largest corporation in the world
CARE	CARE is a major international humanitarian agency delivering broad-spectrum emergency relief and long-term international development projects. Founded in 1945, CARE is nonsectarian, non-partisan, and non-governmental. It is one of the largest and oldest humanitarian aid organizations focused on fighting global poverty.
Health care	Health care is the diagnosis, treatment, and prevention of disease, illness, injury, and other physical and mental impairments in human beings. Health care is delivered by practitioners in allied health, dentistry, midwifery-obstetrics, medicine, nursing, optometry, pharmacy, psychology and other care providers. It refers to the work done in providing primary care, secondary care, and tertiary care, as well as in public health.
Need	A need is something that is necessary for organisms to live a healthy life. Needs are distinguished from wants because a deficiency would cause a clear negative outcome, such as dysfunction or death. Needs can be objective and physical, such as food, or they can be subjective and psychological, such as the need for self-esteem.
Law	A law is a universal principle that describes the fundamental nature of something, the universal properties and the relationships between things, or a description that purports to explain these principles and relationships.
Price	In ordinary usage, price is the quantity of payment or compensation given by one party to another in return for goods or services. In modern economies, prices are generally expressed in units of some form of currency. (For commodities, they are expressed as currency per unit weight of the commodity, e.g. euros per kilogram).
Rationing	Rationing is the controlled distribution of scarce resources, goods, or services. Rationing controls the size of the ration, one's allotted portion of the resources being distributed on a particular day or at a particular time.

Control	Controlling is one of the managerial functions like planning, organizing, staffing and directing. It is an important function because it helps to check the errors and to take the corrective action so that deviation from standards are minimized and stated goals of the organization are achieved in a desired manner. According to modern concepts, control is a foreseeing action whereas earlier concept of control was used only when errors were detected.
Index	In economics and finance, an index is a statistical measure of changes in a representative group of individual data points. These data may be derived from any number of sources, including company performance, prices, productivity, and employment. Economic indices (index, plural) track economic health from different perspectives.
Prescription	In law, prescription is the method of sovereignty transfer of a territory through international law analogous to the common law doctrine of adverse possession for private real-estate. Prescription involves the open encroachment by the new sovereign upon the territory in question for a prolonged period of time, acting as the sovereign, without protest or other contest by the original sovereign. This doctrine legalizes de jure the de facto transfer of sovereignty caused in part by the original sovereign's extended negligence and/or neglect of the area in question.
Price controls	Price controls are governmental restrictions on the prices that can be charged for goods and services in a market. The intent behind implementing such controls can stem from the desire to maintain affordability of staple foods and goods, to prevent price gouging during shortages, and to slow inflation, or, alternatively, to insure a minimum income for providers of certain goods or a minimum wage. There are two primary forms of price control, a price ceiling, the maximum price that can be charged, and a price floor, the minimum price that can be charged.
Price index	A price index is a normalized average of price relatives for a given class of goods or services in a given region, during a given interval of time. It is a statistic designed to help to compare how these price relatives, taken as a whole, differ between time periods or geographical locations. Price indexes have several potential uses.
Economy	An economy or economic system consists of the production, distribution or trade, and consumption of limited goods and services by different agents in a given geographical location. The economic agents can be individuals, businesses, organizations, or governments. Transactions occur when two parties agree to the value or price of the transacted good or service, commonly expressed in a certain currency.
Production	Production is a process of combining various material inputs and immaterial inputs in order to make something for consumption (the output). It is the act of creating output, a good or service which has value and contributes to the utility of individuals.

15. The health policy conundrum

Preference	In economics and other social sciences, preference refers to the set of assumptions related to ordering some alternatives, based on the degree of happiness, satisfaction, gratification, enjoyment, or utility they provide, a process which results in an optimal 'choice' . Although economists are usually not interested in choices or preferences in themselves, they are interested in the theory of choice because it serves as a background for empirical demand analysis.
Health equity	Health equity refers to the study of differences in the quality of health and healthcare across different populations. Health equity is different from health equality, as it refers only to the absence of disparities in controllable or remediable aspects of health. It is not possible to work towards complete equality in health, as there are some factors of health that are beyond human influence.

1. A _____ is something that is necessary for organisms to live a healthy life. _____s are distinguished from wants because a deficiency would cause a clear negative outcome, such as dysfunction or death. _____s can be objective and physical, such as food, or they can be subjective and psychological, such as the _____ for self-esteem.

   a. Base period
   b. Benefit incidence
   c. Blanket order
   d. Need

2. In economics, _____ for a good or service is an entire listing of the quantity of the good or service that a market would choose to buy, for every possible market price of the good or service. (Note: This distinguishes '_____' from 'quantity demanded', where _____ is a listing or graphing of quantity demanded at each possible price. In contrast to _____, quantity demanded is the exact quantity demanded at a certain price.

   a. Budget set
   b. Complementary good
   c. Demand
   d. Consumption

3. . _____ is the equitable transfer of the risk of a loss, from one entity to another in exchange for payment. It is a form of risk management primarily used to hedge against the risk of a contingent, uncertain loss.

According to study texts of The Chartered _____ Institute, there are the following categories of risk:•Financial risks which means that the risk must have financial measurement.•Pure risks which means that the risk must be real and not related to gambling•Particular risks which means that these risks are not widespread in their effect, for example such as earthquake risk for the region prone to it.

It is commonly accepted that only financial, pure and particular risks are insurable.

a. Fuel protests in the United Kingdom
b. Insurance
c. Freikorps Lichtschlag
d. Freikorps Oberland

4. _____ is a skin coloured cosmetic applied to the face to create an even, uniform colour to the complexion, to cover flaws and, sometimes, to change the natural skintone. _____ applied to the body is generally referred to as 'body painting.'

a. Foundation
b. Beauty mark
c. Beauty micrometer
d. Beauty salon

5. In accounting and finance, _____ is the residual claimant or interest of the most junior class of investors in assets, after all liabilities are paid; if liability exceeds assets, negative _____ exists. In an accounting context, shareholders' _____ represents the remaining interest in the assets of a company, spread among individual shareholders of common or preferred stock; a negative shareholders' _____ is often referred to as a positive shareholders' deficit.

At the very start of a business, owners put some funding into the business to finance operations.

a. Equity
b. Barbell strategy
c. BATS Chi-X Europe
d. Bellwether

1. d
2. c
3. b
4. a
5. a

You can take the complete Online Interactive Chapter Practice Test

for 15. The health policy conundrum
on all key terms, persons, places, and concepts.

No Additional Costs

http://www.Cram101.com

Register, send an email request to Travis.Reese@Cram101.com to get your user Id and password.

Include your customer order number, and ISBN number from your studyguide Retailer.

16. The Beveridge model: nationalized health care

_____ Service

_____ CARE

_____ Demand

_____ Health care

_____ Health insurance

_____ Insurance

_____ Public health

_____ Internal market

_____ Market

_____ Medicare

_____ Price

_____ Rationing

_____ Gatekeeping

_____ Welfare

_____ Socioeconomic status

_____ Status

_____ Health technology assessment

_____ Technology assessment

_____ Lottery

_____ Competition

_____ Foundation

16. The Beveridge model: nationalized health care

CHAPTER OUTLINE: KEY TERMS, PEOPLE, PLACES, CONCEPTS

	Trust
	Budget
	MOVE
	Cuba

CHAPTER HIGHLIGHTS & NOTES: KEY TERMS, PEOPLE, PLACES, CONCEPTS

Service	In economics, a service is an intangible commodity. That is, services are an example of intangible economic goods.
	Service provision is often an economic activity where the buyer does not generally, except by exclusive contract, obtain exclusive ownership of the thing purchased.
CARE	CARE is a major international humanitarian agency delivering broad-spectrum emergency relief and long-term international development projects. Founded in 1945, CARE is nonsectarian, non-partisan, and non-governmental. It is one of the largest and oldest humanitarian aid organizations focused on fighting global poverty.
Demand	In economics, demand for a good or service is an entire listing of the quantity of the good or service that a market would choose to buy, for every possible market price of the good or service. (Note: This distinguishes 'demand' from 'quantity demanded', where demand is a listing or graphing of quantity demanded at each possible price. In contrast to demand, quantity demanded is the exact quantity demanded at a certain price.
Health care	Health care is the diagnosis, treatment, and prevention of disease, illness, injury, and other physical and mental impairments in human beings. Health care is delivered by practitioners in allied health, dentistry, midwifery-obstetrics, medicine, nursing, optometry, pharmacy, psychology and other care providers. It refers to the work done in providing primary care, secondary care, and tertiary care, as well as in public health.
Health insurance	Health insurance is insurance against the risk of incurring medical expenses among individuals.

16. The Beveridge model: nationalized health care

	By estimating the overall risk of health care and health system expenses, among a targeted group, an insurer can develop a routine finance structure, such as a monthly premium or payroll tax, to ensure that money is available to pay for the health care benefits specified in the insurance agreement. The benefit is administered by a central organization such as a government agency, private business, or not-for-profit entity.
Insurance	Insurance is the equitable transfer of the risk of a loss, from one entity to another in exchange for payment. It is a form of risk management primarily used to hedge against the risk of a contingent, uncertain loss. According to study texts of The Chartered Insurance Institute, there are the following categories of risk:•Financial risks which means that the risk must have financial measurement.•Pure risks which means that the risk must be real and not related to gambling•Particular risks which means that these risks are not widespread in their effect, for example such as earthquake risk for the region prone to it. It is commonly accepted that only financial, pure and particular risks are insurable.
Public health	Public health is 'the science and art of preventing disease, prolonging life and promoting health through the organized efforts and informed choices of society, organizations, public and private, communities and individuals.' It is concerned with threats to health based on population health analysis. The population in question can be as small as a handful of people, or as large as all the inhabitants of several continents (for instance, in the case of a pandemic). The dimensions of health can encompass 'a state of complete physical, mental and social well-being and not merely the absence of disease or infirmity', as defined by the United Nations' World Health Organization.
Internal market	The European Union's internal market seeks to guarantee the free movement of goods, capital, services, and people - the EU's 'four freedoms' - within the EU's 28 member states. The internal market is intended to be conducive to increased competition, increased specialisation, larger economies of scale, allowing goods and factors of production to move to the area where they are most valued, thus improving the efficiency of the allocation of resources. It is also intended to drive economic integration whereby the once separate economies of the member states become integrated within a single EU wide economy.
Market	A market is one of the many varieties of systems, institutions, procedures, social relations and infrastructures whereby parties engage in exchange. While parties may exchange goods and services by barter, most markets rely on sellers offering their goods or services (including labor) in exchange for money from buyers. It can be said that a market is the process by which the prices of goods and services are established.

Medicare	In the United States, Medicare is a national social insurance program, administered by the U.S. federal government since 1966, that guarantees access to health insurance for Americans aged 65 and older who have worked and paid into the system, and younger people with disabilities as well as people with end stage renal disease (Medicare.gov, 2012) and persons with amyotrophic lateral sclerosis. As a social insurance program, Medicare spreads the financial risk associated with illness across society to protect everyone, and thus has a somewhat different social role from for-profit private insurers, which manage their risk portfolio by adjusting their pricing according to perceived risk. In 2010, Medicare provided health insurance to 48 million Americans--40 million people age 65 and older and eight million younger people with disabilities.
Price	In ordinary usage, price is the quantity of payment or compensation given by one party to another in return for goods or services. In modern economies, prices are generally expressed in units of some form of currency. (For commodities, they are expressed as currency per unit weight of the commodity, e.g. euros per kilogram).
Rationing	Rationing is the controlled distribution of scarce resources, goods, or services. Rationing controls the size of the ration, one's allotted portion of the resources being distributed on a particular day or at a particular time.
Gatekeeping	Gatekeeping is the process through which information is filtered for dissemination, whether for publication, broadcasting, the Internet, or some other mode of communication. The academic theory of gatekeeping is found in multiple fields of study, including communication studies, journalism, political science, and sociology. It was originally focused on the mass media with its few-to-many dynamic but now gatekeeping theory also addresses face-to-face communication and the many-to-many dynamic inherent in the Internet.
Welfare	Welfare is the provision of a minimal level of well-being and social support for all citizens, sometimes referred to as public aid. In most developed countries welfare is largely provided by the government, and to a lesser extent, charities, informal social groups, religious groups, and inter-governmental organizations. The welfare state expands on this concept to include services such as universal healthcare and unemployment insurance.
Socioeconomic status	Socioeconomic status is an economic and sociological combined total measure of a person's work experience and of an individual's or family's economic and social position in relation to others, based on income, education, and occupation.

16. The Beveridge model: nationalized health care

CHAPTER HIGHLIGHTS & NOTES: KEY TERMS, PEOPLE, PLACES, CONCEPTS

	When analyzing a family's SES, the household income, earners' education, and occupation are examined, as well as combined income, versus with an individual, when their own attributes are assessed.
	Socioeconomic status is typically broken into three categories, high SES, middle SES, and low SES to describe the three areas a family or an individual may fall into.
Status	An Individual's status is a legal position held in regards to the rest of the community and not by an act of law or by the consensual acts of the parties, and it is in rem, i.e. these conditions must be recognised by the world. It is the qualities of universality and permanence that distinguish status from consensual relationships such as employment and agency. Hence, a person's status and its attributes are set by the law of the domicile if born in a common law state, or by the law of nationality if born in a civil law state and this status and its attendant capacities should be recognised wherever the person may later travel.
Health technology assessment	Health technology assessment is a multi-disciplinary field of policy analysis that studies the medical, social, ethical, and economic implications of development, diffusion, and use of health technology. It has other definitions including 'the systematic evaluation of the properties and effects of a health technology, addressing the direct and intended effects of this technology, as well as its indirect and unintended consequences, and aimed mainly at informing decision making regarding health technologies.' and 'a multidisciplinary process that summarises information about the medical, social, economic and ethical issues related to the use of a health technology in a systematic, transparent, unbiased, robust manner. Its aim is to inform the formulation of safe, effective, health policies that are patient focused and seek to achieve best value.
Technology assessment	Technology assessment is a scientific, interactive, and communicative process that aims to contribute to the formation of public and political opinion on societal aspects of science and technology.
Lottery	In expected utility theory, a lottery is a discrete distribution of probability on a set of states of nature. The elements of a lottery correspond to the probability that a certain outcome arises from a given state of nature. In economics, individuals are assumed to rank lotteries according to a rational system of preferences, although it is now accepted that people make irrational choices systematically.
Competition	In economics, competition is the rivalry among sellers trying to achieve such goals as increasing profits, market share, and sales volume by varying the elements of the marketing mix: price, product, distribution, and promotion. Merriam-Webster defines competition in business as 'the effort of two or more parties acting independently to secure the business of a third party by offering the most favorable terms.' It was described by Adam Smith in The Wealth of Nations (1776) and later economists as allocating productive resources to their most highly-valued uses and encouraging efficiency.

16. The Beveridge model: nationalized health care

Foundation	Foundation is a skin coloured cosmetic applied to the face to create an even, uniform colour to the complexion, to cover flaws and, sometimes, to change the natural skintone. Foundation applied to the body is generally referred to as 'body painting.'
Trust	A 'trust,' or 'corporate trust' means a large business. Originally, it was Standard Oil, which was already the largest corporation in the world
Budget	A budget is a quantitative expression of a plan for a defined period of time. It may include planned sales volumes and revenues, resource quantities, costs and expenses, assets, liabilities and cash flows. It expresses strategic plans of business units, organizations, activities or events in measurable terms.
MOVE	MOVE or the MOVE Organization is a Philadelphia-based black liberation group founded by John Africa. MOVE was described by CNN as 'a loose-knit, mostly black group whose members all adopted the surname Africa, advocated a 'back-to-nature' lifestyle and preached against technology'. The group lived communally and frequently engaged in public demonstrations related to issues they deemed important. Since their founding in 1972, MOVE has been in frequent conflict with the Philadelphia Police Department.
Cuba	Cuba, officially the Republic of Cuba is an island country in the Caribbean. The nation of Cuba comprises the main island of Cuba, the Isla de la Juventud, and several archipelagos. Havana is the capital of Cuba and its largest city.

1. _____ is insurance against the risk of incurring medical expenses among individuals. By estimating the overall risk of health care and health system expenses, among a targeted group, an insurer can develop a routine finance structure, such as a monthly premium or payroll tax, to ensure that money is available to pay for the health care benefits specified in the insurance agreement. The benefit is administered by a central organization such as a government agency, private business, or not-for-profit entity.

   a. Health insurance
   b. Capitation
   c. Case mix group
   d. Centre for Reviews and Dissemination

2. . In economics, _____ for a good or service is an entire listing of the quantity of the good or service that a market would choose to buy, for every possible market price of the good or service. (Note: This distinguishes '_____' from 'quantity demanded', where _____ is a listing or graphing of quantity demanded at each possible price.

In contrast to _____, quantity demanded is the exact quantity demanded at a certain price.

a. Demand
b. Complementary good
c. Consumer service
d. Consumption

3. _____ is 'the science and art of preventing disease, prolonging life and promoting health through the organized efforts and informed choices of society, organizations, public and private, communities and individuals.' It is concerned with threats to health based on population health analysis. The population in question can be as small as a handful of people, or as large as all the inhabitants of several continents (for instance, in the case of a pandemic). The dimensions of health can encompass 'a state of complete physical, mental and social well-being and not merely the absence of disease or infirmity', as defined by the United Nations' World Health Organization.

a. Bundled payment
b. Public health
c. Case mix group
d. Centre for Reviews and Dissemination

4. _____ is the equitable transfer of the risk of a loss, from one entity to another in exchange for payment. It is a form of risk management primarily used to hedge against the risk of a contingent, uncertain loss.

According to study texts of The Chartered _____ Institute, there are the following categories of risk:•Financial risks which means that the risk must have financial measurement.•Pure risks which means that the risk must be real and not related to gambling•Particular risks which means that these risks are not widespread in their effect, for example such as earthquake risk for the region prone to it.

It is commonly accepted that only financial, pure and particular risks are insurable.

a. Insurance
b. Battle of Annaberg
c. Freikorps Lichtschlag
d. Freikorps Oberland

5. . In economics, a _____ is an intangible commodity. That is, _____s are an example of intangible economic goods.

_____ provision is often an economic activity where the buyer does not generally, except by exclusive contract, obtain exclusive ownership of the thing purchased.

a. Base period
b. Service
c. Blanket order

1. a
2. a
3. b
4. a
5. b

You can take the complete Online Interactive Chapter Practice Test

for 16. The Beveridge model: nationalized health care
on all key terms, persons, places, and concepts.

No Additional Costs

http://www.Cram101.com

Register, send an email request to Travis.Reese@Cram101.com to get your user Id and password.

Include your customer order number, and ISBN number from your studyguide Retailer.

CHAPTER OUTLINE: KEY TERMS, PEOPLE, PLACES, CONCEPTS

Community rating

Health insurance

Insurance

Price

Rationing

Competition

Market

Medicare

Cream skimming

Demand

Model risk

Skimming

Adverse selection

Oligopoly

Control

Price controls

Schedule

China

Distortion

Prescription

Coase theorem

17. The Bismarck model: social health insurance

CHAPTER OUTLINE: KEY TERMS, PEOPLE, PLACES, CONCEPTS

	Consumer
	Innovation
	Pharmaceutical industry
	Access
	Gatekeeping
	Internal market

CHAPTER HIGHLIGHTS & NOTES: KEY TERMS, PEOPLE, PLACES, CONCEPTS

Community rating	Community rating is a concept usually associated with health insurance, which requires health insurance providers to offer health insurance policies within a given territory at the same price to all persons without medical underwriting, regardless of their health status. Pure community rating prohibits insurance rate variations based on demographic characteristics such as age or gender, whereas adjusted or modified community rating allows insurance rate variations based on demographic characteristics such as age or gender.
Health insurance	Health insurance is insurance against the risk of incurring medical expenses among individuals. By estimating the overall risk of health care and health system expenses, among a targeted group, an insurer can develop a routine finance structure, such as a monthly premium or payroll tax, to ensure that money is available to pay for the health care benefits specified in the insurance agreement. The benefit is administered by a central organization such as a government agency, private business, or not-for-profit entity.
Insurance	Insurance is the equitable transfer of the risk of a loss, from one entity to another in exchange for payment. It is a form of risk management primarily used to hedge against the risk of a contingent, uncertain loss.

| | According to study texts of The Chartered Insurance Institute, there are the following categories of risk:•Financial risks which means that the risk must have financial measurement.•Pure risks which means that the risk must be real and not related to gambling•Particular risks which means that these risks are not widespread in their effect, for example such as earthquake risk for the region prone to it.

It is commonly accepted that only financial, pure and particular risks are insurable. |
|---|---|
| Price | In ordinary usage, price is the quantity of payment or compensation given by one party to another in return for goods or services.

In modern economies, prices are generally expressed in units of some form of currency. (For commodities, they are expressed as currency per unit weight of the commodity, e.g. euros per kilogram). |
Rationing	Rationing is the controlled distribution of scarce resources, goods, or services. Rationing controls the size of the ration, one's allotted portion of the resources being distributed on a particular day or at a particular time.
Competition	In economics, competition is the rivalry among sellers trying to achieve such goals as increasing profits, market share, and sales volume by varying the elements of the marketing mix: price, product, distribution, and promotion. Merriam-Webster defines competition in business as 'the effort of two or more parties acting independently to secure the business of a third party by offering the most favorable terms.' It was described by Adam Smith in The Wealth of Nations (1776) and later economists as allocating productive resources to their most highly-valued uses and encouraging efficiency. Smith and other classical economists before Cournot were referring to price and non-price rivalry among producers to sell their goods on best terms by bidding of buyers, not necessarily to a large number of sellers nor to a market in final equilibrium.
Market	A market is one of the many varieties of systems, institutions, procedures, social relations and infrastructures whereby parties engage in exchange. While parties may exchange goods and services by barter, most markets rely on sellers offering their goods or services (including labor) in exchange for money from buyers. It can be said that a market is the process by which the prices of goods and services are established.
Medicare	In the United States, Medicare is a national social insurance program, administered by the U.S. federal government since 1966, that guarantees access to health insurance for Americans aged 65 and older who have worked and paid into the system, and younger people with disabilities as well as people with end stage renal disease (Medicare.gov, 2012) and persons with amyotrophic lateral sclerosis.

17. The Bismarck model: social health insurance

	As a social insurance program, Medicare spreads the financial risk associated with illness across society to protect everyone, and thus has a somewhat different social role from for-profit private insurers, which manage their risk portfolio by adjusting their pricing according to perceived risk.
	In 2010, Medicare provided health insurance to 48 million Americans--40 million people age 65 and older and eight million younger people with disabilities.
Cream skimming	Cream skimming is a pejorative conceptual metaphor used to refer to the perceived business practice of a company providing a product or a service to only the high-value or low-cost customers of that product or service.
	The term derives from the practice of extracting cream from fresh milk at a dairy, in which a separator draws off the cream from fresh or raw milk. The cream has now been 'skimmed' or captured separately from the fresh milk.
Demand	In economics, demand for a good or service is an entire listing of the quantity of the good or service that a market would choose to buy, for every possible market price of the good or service. (Note: This distinguishes 'demand' from 'quantity demanded', where demand is a listing or graphing of quantity demanded at each possible price. In contrast to demand, quantity demanded is the exact quantity demanded at a certain price.
Model risk	In finance, model risk is the risk of loss resulting from using models to make decisions, initially and frequently referring to valuing financial securities. However model risk is more and more prevalent in industries other than financial securities valuation, such as consumer credit score, real-time probability prediction of a fradulent credit card transaction to the probability of air flight passenger being a terrorist. Rebonato in 2002 considers alternative definitions including:•After observing a set of prices for the underlying and hedging instruments, different but identically calibrated models might produce different prices for the same exotic product.•Losses will be incurred because of an 'incorrect' hedging strategy suggested by a model.
	Rebonato defines model risk as 'the risk of occurrence of a significant difference between the mark-to-model value of a complex and/or illiquid instrument, and the price at which the same instrument is revealed to have traded in the market.'
Skimming	A form of white-collar crime, skimming is a slang term that refers to taking cash 'off the top' of the daily receipts of a business and officially reporting a lower total; the formal legal term is defalcation.
Adverse selection	Adverse selection, anti-selection, or negative selection is a term used in economics, insurance, risk management, and statistics. It refers to a market process in which undesired results occur when buyers and sellers have asymmetric information (access to different information); the 'bad' products or services are more likely to be selected.

Oligopoly	An oligopoly is a market form in which a market or industry is dominated by a small number of sellers . Oligopolies can result from various forms of collusion which reduce competition and lead to higher prices for consumers. With few sellers, each oligopolist is likely to be aware of the actions of the others.
Control	Controlling is one of the managerial functions like planning, organizing, staffing and directing. It is an important function because it helps to check the errors and to take the corrective action so that deviation from standards are minimized and stated goals of the organization are achieved in a desired manner. According to modern concepts, control is a foreseeing action whereas earlier concept of control was used only when errors were detected.
Price controls	Price controls are governmental restrictions on the prices that can be charged for goods and services in a market. The intent behind implementing such controls can stem from the desire to maintain affordability of staple foods and goods, to prevent price gouging during shortages, and to slow inflation, or, alternatively, to insure a minimum income for providers of certain goods or a minimum wage. There are two primary forms of price control, a price ceiling, the maximum price that can be charged, and a price floor, the minimum price that can be charged.
Schedule	A schedule, often called a rota or roster, is a list of employees who are working on any given day, week, or month in a workplace. A schedule is necessary for the day-to-day operation of any retail store, manufacturing facility and some offices. The process of creating a schedule is called scheduling.
China	China, officially the People's Republic of China, is a sovereign state located in East Asia. It is the world's most populous country, with a population of over 1.35 billion. The PRC is a single-party state governed by the Communist Party, with its seat of government in the capital city of Beijing.
Distortion	A distortion is departure from the allocation of economic resources from the state in which each agent maximizes his/her own welfare. A proportional wage-income tax, for instance, is distortionary, whereas a lump-sum tax is not. In a competitive equilibrium, a proportional wage income tax discourages work.
Prescription	In law, prescription is the method of sovereignty transfer of a territory through international law analogous to the common law doctrine of adverse possession for private real-estate. Prescription involves the open encroachment by the new sovereign upon the territory in question for a prolonged period of time, acting as the sovereign, without protest or other contest by the original sovereign. This doctrine legalizes de jure the de facto transfer of sovereignty caused in part by the original sovereign's extended negligence and/or neglect of the area in question.

17. The Bismarck model: social health insurance

Coase theorem	In law and economics, the Coase theorem describes the economic efficiency of an economic allocation or outcome in the presence of externalities. The theorem states that if trade in an externality is possible and there are sufficiently low transaction costs, bargaining will lead to an efficient outcome regardless of the initial allocation of property. In practice, obstacles to bargaining or poorly defined property rights can prevent Coasian bargaining.
Consumer	A consumer is a person or group of people, such as a household, who are the final users of products or services. The consumer's use is final in the sense that the product is usually not improved by the use.
Innovation	Innovation is the application of better solutions that meet new requirements, in-articulated needs, or existing market needs. This is accomplished through more effective products, processes, services, technologies, or ideas that are readily available to markets, governments and society. The term innovation can be defined as something original and, as a consequence, new, that 'breaks into' the market or society.
Pharmaceutical industry	The pharmaceutical industry develops, produces, and markets drugs or pharmaceuticals licensed for use as medications. Pharmaceutical companies are allowed to deal in generic or brand medications and medical devices. They are subject to a variety of laws and regulations regarding the patenting, testing and ensuring safety and efficacy and marketing of drugs.
Access	Access is a catalytic process that enables interactions, contact and exchanges among people, businesses and nations. An analytical framework to define the drivers and benefits of Access and to quantify the impact of Access on economic growth and personal well-being was created in 2006 by the Center for Science, Technology, and Economic Development at SRI International (formerly known as the Stanford Research Institute) in its study, "The Power of Access" (also titled, "How Greater Access Is Changing The World: A Landmark Study on the Relevance of Access to People, Businesses and Nations"). As outlined in the study, the Access framework consists of the Access Model, which expresses the function of Access as an econometric equation; the "Access Cycle"; and the 'Access Index,' which ranks 75 nations based on their performance in 22 metrics, including transportation infrastructure; telecommunications networks; trade policy; and news, media and information services.
Gatekeeping	Gatekeeping is the process through which information is filtered for dissemination, whether for publication, broadcasting, the Internet, or some other mode of communication. The academic theory of gatekeeping is found in multiple fields of study, including communication studies, journalism, political science, and sociology. It was originally focused on the mass media with its few-to-many dynamic but now gatekeeping theory also addresses face-to-face communication and the many-to-many dynamic inherent in the Internet.
Internal market	The European Union's internal market seeks to guarantee the free movement of goods, capital, services, and people - the EU's 'four freedoms' - within the EU's 28 member states.

The internal market is intended to be conducive to increased competition, increased specialisation, larger economies of scale, allowing goods and factors of production to move to the area where they are most valued, thus improving the efficiency of the allocation of resources.

It is also intended to drive economic integration whereby the once separate economies of the member states become integrated within a single EU wide economy.

1. In finance, _____ is the risk of loss resulting from using models to make decisions, initially and frequently referring to valuing financial securities. However _____ is more and more prevalent in industries other than financial securities valuation, such as consumer credit score, real-time probability prediction of a fradulent credit card transaction to the probability of air flight passenger being a terrorist. Rebonato in 2002 considers alternative definitions including:•After observing a set of prices for the underlying and hedging instruments, different but identically calibrated models might produce different prices for the same exotic product.•Losses will be incurred because of an 'incorrect' hedging strategy suggested by a model.

   Rebonato defines _____ as 'the risk of occurrence of a significant difference between the mark-to-model value of a complex and/or illiquid instrument, and the price at which the same instrument is revealed to have traded in the market.'

   a. Bailout
   b. Basis risk
   c. Capital Requirements Directive
   d. Model risk

2. . _____ is a concept usually associated with health insurance, which requires health insurance providers to offer health insurance policies within a given territory at the same price to all persons without medical underwriting, regardless of their health status.

   Pure _____ prohibits insurance rate variations based on demographic characteristics such as age or gender, whereas adjusted or modified _____ allows insurance rate variations based on demographic characteristics such as age or gender.

   a. Community rating
   b. Case mix group
   c. Centre for Reviews and Dissemination

17. The Bismarck model: social health insurance

3. _____ is insurance against the risk of incurring medical expenses among individuals. By estimating the overall risk of health care and health system expenses, among a targeted group, an insurer can develop a routine finance structure, such as a monthly premium or payroll tax, to ensure that money is available to pay for the health care benefits specified in the insurance agreement. The benefit is administered by a central organization such as a government agency, private business, or not-for-profit entity.

   a. Health insurance
   b. Capitation
   c. Case mix group
   d. Centre for Reviews and Dissemination

4. In ordinary usage, _____ is the quantity of payment or compensation given by one party to another in return for goods or services.

   In modern economies, _____s are generally expressed in units of some form of currency. (For commodities, they are expressed as currency per unit weight of the commodity, e.g. euros per kilogram).

   a. Balloon payment mortgage
   b. Price
   c. Collateral
   d. Compound annual growth rate

5. A _____ is one of the many varieties of systems, institutions, procedures, social relations and infrastructures whereby parties engage in exchange. While parties may exchange goods and services by barter, most _____s rely on sellers offering their goods or services (including labor) in exchange for money from buyers. It can be said that a _____ is the process by which the prices of goods and services are established.

   a. Financial market
   b. Market
   c. Battle of Annaberg
   d. Freikorps Lichtschlag

ANSWER KEY
17. The Bismarck model: social health insurance

---

1. d
2. a
3. a
4. b
5. b

You can take the complete Online Interactive Chapter Practice Test

for 17. The Bismarck model: social health insurance
on all key terms, persons, places, and concepts.

No Additional Costs

http://www.Cram101.com

Register, send an email request to Travis.Reese@Cram101.com to get your user Id and password.

Include your customer order number, and ISBN number from your studyguide Retailer.

CHAPTER OUTLINE: KEY TERMS, PEOPLE, PLACES, CONCEPTS

	CARE
	Demand
	Health care
	Insurance
	Price
	Rationing
	Capital
	Human capital
	Wage
	Health insurance
	Adverse selection
	Market
	Job lock
	Budget
	Fee-for-service
	Managed care
	Medicare
	Preferred provider organization
	Effectiveness
	Control
	Medicaid

18. The American model

	Structuring
	Community rating

CARE	CARE is a major international humanitarian agency delivering broad-spectrum emergency relief and long-term international development projects. Founded in 1945, CARE is nonsectarian, non-partisan, and non-governmental. It is one of the largest and oldest humanitarian aid organizations focused on fighting global poverty.
Demand	In economics, demand for a good or service is an entire listing of the quantity of the good or service that a market would choose to buy, for every possible market price of the good or service. (Note: This distinguishes 'demand' from 'quantity demanded', where demand is a listing or graphing of quantity demanded at each possible price. In contrast to demand, quantity demanded is the exact quantity demanded at a certain price.
Health care	Health care is the diagnosis, treatment, and prevention of disease, illness, injury, and other physical and mental impairments in human beings. Health care is delivered by practitioners in allied health, dentistry, midwifery-obstetrics, medicine, nursing, optometry, pharmacy, psychology and other care providers. It refers to the work done in providing primary care, secondary care, and tertiary care, as well as in public health.
Insurance	Insurance is the equitable transfer of the risk of a loss, from one entity to another in exchange for payment. It is a form of risk management primarily used to hedge against the risk of a contingent, uncertain loss. According to study texts of The Chartered Insurance Institute, there are the following categories of risk:•Financial risks which means that the risk must have financial measurement.•Pure risks which means that the risk must be real and not related to gambling•Particular risks which means that these risks are not widespread in their effect, for example such as earthquake risk for the region prone to it. It is commonly accepted that only financial, pure and particular risks are insurable.
Price	In ordinary usage, price is the quantity of payment or compensation given by one party to another in return for goods or services.

	In modern economies, prices are generally expressed in units of some form of currency. (For commodities, they are expressed as currency per unit weight of the commodity, e.g. euros per kilogram).
Rationing	Rationing is the controlled distribution of scarce resources, goods, or services. Rationing controls the size of the ration, one's allotted portion of the resources being distributed on a particular day or at a particular time.
Capital	In economics, capital goods, real capital, or capital assets are already-produced durable goods or any non-financial asset that is used in production of goods or services.
	Capital goods are not significantly consumed in the production process though they may depreciate. How a capital good or is maintained or returned to its pre-production state varies with the type of capital involved.
Human capital	Human capital is the stock of competencies, knowledge, habits, social and personality attributes, including creativity, cognitive abilities, embodied in the ability to perform labor so as to produce economic value. It is an aggregate economic view of the human being acting within economies, which is an attempt to capture the social, biological, cultural and psychological complexity as they interact in explicit and/or economic transactions. Many theories explicitly connect investment in human capital development to education, and the role of human capital in economic development, productivity growth, and innovation has frequently been cited as a justification for government subsidies for education and job skills training.
Wage	A wage is monetary compensation paid by an employer to an employee in exchange for work done. Payment may be calculated as a fixed amount for each task completed (a task wage or piece rate), or at an hourly or daily rate, or based on an easily measured quantity of work done.
	Payment by wage contrasts with salaried work, in which the employer pays an arranged amount at steady intervals (such as a week or month) regardless of hours worked, with commission which conditions pay on individual performance, and with compensation based on the performance of the company as a whole.
Health insurance	Health insurance is insurance against the risk of incurring medical expenses among individuals. By estimating the overall risk of health care and health system expenses, among a targeted group, an insurer can develop a routine finance structure, such as a monthly premium or payroll tax, to ensure that money is available to pay for the health care benefits specified in the insurance agreement. The benefit is administered by a central organization such as a government agency, private business, or not-for-profit entity.

18. The American model

Adverse selection	Adverse selection, anti-selection, or negative selection is a term used in economics, insurance, risk management, and statistics. It refers to a market process in which undesired results occur when buyers and sellers have asymmetric information (access to different information); the 'bad' products or services are more likely to be selected. For example, a bank that sets one price for all of its checking account customers runs the risk of being adversely selected against by its low-balance, high-activity (and hence least profitable) customers.
Market	A market is one of the many varieties of systems, institutions, procedures, social relations and infrastructures whereby parties engage in exchange. While parties may exchange goods and services by barter, most markets rely on sellers offering their goods or services (including labor) in exchange for money from buyers. It can be said that a market is the process by which the prices of goods and services are established.
Job lock	The term job lock is used to describe the inability of an employee to freely leave a job because doing so will result in the loss of employee benefits . In a broader sense, job lock may describe the situation where an employee is being paid higher than scale or has accumulated significant benefits, so that changing jobs is not a realistic option as it would result in significantly lower pay, less vacation time, etc.
Budget	A budget is a quantitative expression of a plan for a defined period of time. It may include planned sales volumes and revenues, resource quantities, costs and expenses, assets, liabilities and cash flows. It expresses strategic plans of business units, organizations, activities or events in measurable terms.
Fee-for-service	Fee-for-service is a payment model where services are unbundled and paid for separately. In health care, it gives an incentive for physicians to provide more treatments because payment is dependent on the quantity of care, rather than quality of care. Similarly, when patients are shielded from paying (cost-sharing) by health insurance coverage, they are incentivized to welcome any medical service that might do some good.
Managed care	The term managed care or managed health care is used in the United States to describe a variety of techniques intended to reduce the cost of providing health benefits and improve the quality of care ('managed care techniques'), for organizations that use those techniques or provide them as services to other organizations ('managed care organization' or 'MCO'), or to describe systems of financing and delivering health care to enrollees organized around managed care techniques and concepts ('managed care delivery systems').

	...intended to reduce unnecessary health care costs through a variety of mechanisms, including: economic incentives for physicians and patients to select less costly forms of care; programs for reviewing the medical necessity of specific services; increased beneficiary cost sharing; controls on inpatient admissions and lengths of stay; the establishment of cost-sharing incentives for outpatient surgery; selective contracting with health care providers; and the intensive management of high-cost health care cases. The programs may be provided in a variety of settings, such as Health Maintenance Organizations and Preferred Provider Organizations.
Medicare	In the United States, Medicare is a national social insurance program, administered by the U.S. federal government since 1966, that guarantees access to health insurance for Americans aged 65 and older who have worked and paid into the system, and younger people with disabilities as well as people with end stage renal disease (Medicare.gov, 2012) and persons with amyotrophic lateral sclerosis. As a social insurance program, Medicare spreads the financial risk associated with illness across society to protect everyone, and thus has a somewhat different social role from for-profit private insurers, which manage their risk portfolio by adjusting their pricing according to perceived risk. In 2010, Medicare provided health insurance to 48 million Americans--40 million people age 65 and older and eight million younger people with disabilities.
Preferred provider organization	In health insurance in the United States, a preferred provider organization is a managed care organization of medical doctors, hospitals, and other health care providers who have agreed with an insurer or a third-party administrator to provide health care at reduced rates to the insurer's or administrator's clients.
Effectiveness	Effectiveness is the capability of producing a desired result. When something is deemed effective, it means it has an intended or expected outcome, or produces a deep, vivid impression.
Control	Controlling is one of the managerial functions like planning, organizing, staffing and directing. It is an important function because it helps to check the errors and to take the corrective action so that deviation from standards are minimized and stated goals of the organization are achieved in a desired manner. According to modern concepts, control is a foreseeing action whereas earlier concept of control was used only when errors were detected.
Medicaid	Medicaid in the United States is a social health care program for families and individuals with low income and resources. The Health Insurance Association of America describes Medicaid as a 'government insurance program for persons of all ages whose income and resources are insufficient to pay for health care.' (America's Health Insurance Plans (HIAA), pg. 232).

18. The American model

Structuring	Structuring, also known as smurfing in banking industry jargon, is the practice of executing financial transactions in a specific pattern calculated to avoid the creation of certain records and reports required by law, such as the United States's Bank Secrecy Act (BSA) and Internal Revenue Code section 6050I (relating to the requirement to file Form 8300).
	Legal restrictions on structuring should not be confused with capital controls, which are statutory or regulatory limits on the money that one can take out of a nation, though they can have some of the same economic effects in some economies, as structuring controls effectively limit the flow of capital by magnitude and duration, and can apply equally to taking money out of a nation as well as putting money into its finance system.
Community rating	Community rating is a concept usually associated with health insurance, which requires health insurance providers to offer health insurance policies within a given territory at the same price to all persons without medical underwriting, regardless of their health status.
	Pure community rating prohibits insurance rate variations based on demographic characteristics such as age or gender, whereas adjusted or modified community rating allows insurance rate variations based on demographic characteristics such as age or gender.

1. _____ is insurance against the risk of incurring medical expenses among individuals. By estimating the overall risk of health care and health system expenses, among a targeted group, an insurer can develop a routine finance structure, such as a monthly premium or payroll tax, to ensure that money is available to pay for the health care benefits specified in the insurance agreement. The benefit is administered by a central organization such as a government agency, private business, or not-for-profit entity.

   a. Health insurance
   b. Capitation
   c. Case mix group
   d. Centre for Reviews and Dissemination

2. . A _____ is monetary compensation paid by an employer to an employee in exchange for work done. Payment may be calculated as a fixed amount for each task completed (a task _____ or piece rate), or at an hourly or daily rate, or based on an easily measured quantity of work done.

Payment by _____ contrasts with salaried work, in which the employer pays an arranged amount at steady intervals (such as a week or month) regardless of hours worked, with commission which conditions pay on individual performance, and with compensation based on the performance of the company as a whole.

a. Wage
b. Compa-ratio
c. Corporate child care
d. Cost to company

3. In ordinary usage, _____ is the quantity of payment or compensation given by one party to another in return for goods or services.

In modern economies, _____s are generally expressed in units of some form of currency. (For commodities, they are expressed as currency per unit weight of the commodity, e.g. euros per kilogram).

a. Balloon payment mortgage
b. Price
c. Collateral
d. Compound annual growth rate

4. _____ is the stock of competencies, knowledge, habits, social and personality attributes, including creativity, cognitive abilities, embodied in the ability to perform labor so as to produce economic value. It is an aggregate economic view of the human being acting within economies, which is an attempt to capture the social, biological, cultural and psychological complexity as they interact in explicit and/or economic transactions. Many theories explicitly connect investment in _____ development to education, and the role of _____ in economic development, productivity growth, and innovation has frequently been cited as a justification for government subsidies for education and job skills training.

a. Capital deepening
b. Capital flight
c. Human capital
d. Capital intensity

5. . _____, also known as smurfing in banking industry jargon, is the practice of executing financial transactions in a specific pattern calculated to avoid the creation of certain records and reports required by law, such as the United States's Bank Secrecy Act (BSA) and Internal Revenue Code section 6050I (relating to the requirement to file Form 8300).

Legal restrictions on _____ should not be confused with capital controls, which are statutory or regulatory limits on the money that one can take out of a nation, though they can have some of the same economic effects in some economies, as _____ controls effectively limit the flow of capital by magnitude and duration, and can apply equally to taking money out of a nation as well as putting money into its finance system.

a. Central Economic Intelligence Bureau

b. Structuring

c. David Wynn Miller

d. Directorate General of Anti-Evasion

ANSWER KEY
18. The American model

1. a
2. a
3. b
4. c
5. b

You can take the complete Online Interactive Chapter Practice Test

for 18. The American model
on all key terms, persons, places, and concepts.

No Additional Costs

http://www.Cram101.com

Register, send an email request to Travis.Reese@Cram101.com to get your user Id and password.

Include your customer order number, and ISBN number from your studyguide Retailer.

CHAPTER OUTLINE: KEY TERMS, PEOPLE, PLACES, CONCEPTS

	Medicare
	Chernobyl disaster
	Committee
	Child mortality
	Life expectancy
	Population pyramid
	Hypothesis
	Income
	Security
	CARE
	Health care
	Trust
	Baby boom
	Insurance
	Price
	Health insurance
	Problem
	End-of-life
	Orphan drug
	Tropical disease
	Cuba

19. Population aging and the future of health policy

CHAPTER HIGHLIGHTS & NOTES: KEY TERMS, PEOPLE, PLACES, CONCEPTS

Medicare	In the United States, Medicare is a national social insurance program, administered by the U.S. federal government since 1966, that guarantees access to health insurance for Americans aged 65 and older who have worked and paid into the system, and younger people with disabilities as well as people with end stage renal disease (Medicare.gov, 2012) and persons with amyotrophic lateral sclerosis. As a social insurance program, Medicare spreads the financial risk associated with illness across society to protect everyone, and thus has a somewhat different social role from for-profit private insurers, which manage their risk portfolio by adjusting their pricing according to perceived risk. In 2010, Medicare provided health insurance to 48 million Americans--40 million people age 65 and older and eight million younger people with disabilities.
Chernobyl disaster	The Chernobyl disaster was a catastrophic nuclear accident that occurred on 26 April 1986 at the Chernobyl Nuclear Power Plant in Ukraine (then officially the Ukrainian SSR), which was under the direct jurisdiction of the central authorities of the Soviet Union. An explosion and fire released large quantities of radioactive particles into the atmosphere, which spread over much of the western USSR and Europe. The Chernobyl disaster is the worst nuclear power plant accident in history in terms of cost and resulting deaths, and is one of only two classified as a level 7 event (the maximum classification) on the International Nuclear Event Scale (the other being the Fukushima Daiichi nuclear disaster in 2011).
Committee	A committee is a type of small deliberative assembly that is usually intended to remain subordinate to another, larger deliberative assembly--which when organized so that action on committee requires a vote by all its entitled members, is called the 'Committee of the Whole'. Committees often serve several different functions:•Governance: in organizations considered too large for all the members to participate in decisions affecting the organization as a whole, a committee is given the power to make decisions, spend money, or take actions. Some or all such powers may be limited or effectively unlimited.
Child mortality	Child mortality, also known as under-5 mortality, refers to the death of infants and children under the age of five. In 2012, 6.6 million, 2011, 6.9 million children under five died, down from 7.6 million in 2010, 8.1 million in 2009, and 12.4 million in 1990. About half of child deaths occur in Sub-Saharan Africa. Reduction of child mortality is the fourth of the United Nations' Millennium Development Goals. Child Mortality Rate is the highest in low-income countries, such as most countries in Sub-Saharan Africa. A child's death is emotionally and physically damaging for the mourning parents.
Life expectancy	Life expectancy is the expected number of years of life remaining at a given age. It is denoted by e_x , which means the average number of subsequent years of life for someone now aged

x , according to a particular mortality experience. Because life expectancy is an average, a particular person may well die many years before or many years after their 'expected' survival.

Population pyramid	A population pyramid, also called an age pyramid or age picture diagram, is a graphical illustration that shows the distribution of various age groups in a population, which forms the shape of a pyramid when the population is growing. It is also used in ecology to determine the overall age distribution of a population; an indication of the reproductive capabilities and likelihood of the continuation of a species. It typically consists of two back-to-back bar graphs, with the population plotted on the X-axis and age on the Y-axis, one showing the number of males and one showing females in a particular population in five-year age groups (also called cohorts).
Hypothesis	A hypothesis is a proposed explanation for a phenomenon. For a hypothesis to be a scientific hypothesis, the scientific method requires that one can test it. Scientists generally base scientific hypotheses on previous observations that cannot satisfactorily be explained with the available scientific theories.
Income	Income is the consumption and savings opportunity gained by an entity within a specified timeframe, which is generally expressed in monetary terms. However, for households and individuals, 'income is the sum of all the wages, salaries, profits, interests payments, rents and other forms of earnings received... in a given period of time.' In the field of public economics, the term may refer to the accumulation of both monetary and non-monetary consumption ability, with the former (monetary) being used as a proxy for total income.
Security	A security is a tradable asset of any kind. Securities are broadly categorized into:•debt securities (such as banknotes, bonds and debentures),•equity securities, e.g., common stocks; and,•derivative contracts, such as forwards, futures, options and swaps. The company or other entity issuing the security is called the issuer. A country's regulatory structure determines what qualifies as a security.
CARE	CARE is a major international humanitarian agency delivering broad-spectrum emergency relief and long-term international development projects. Founded in 1945, CARE is nonsectarian, non-partisan, and non-governmental. It is one of the largest and oldest humanitarian aid organizations focused on fighting global poverty.
Health care	Health care is the diagnosis, treatment, and prevention of disease, illness, injury, and other physical and mental impairments in human beings. Health care is delivered by practitioners in allied health, dentistry, midwifery-obstetrics, medicine, nursing, optometry, pharmacy, psychology and other care providers.

19. Population aging and the future of health policy

Trust	A 'trust,' or 'corporate trust' means a large business. Originally, it was Standard Oil, which was already the largest corporation in the world
Baby boom	A baby boom is any period marked by a greatly increased birth rate. This demographic phenomenon is usually ascribed within certain geographical bounds. People born during such a period are often called baby boomers; however, some experts distinguish between those born during such demographic baby booms and those who identify with the overlapping cultural generations.
Insurance	Insurance is the equitable transfer of the risk of a loss, from one entity to another in exchange for payment. It is a form of risk management primarily used to hedge against the risk of a contingent, uncertain loss. According to study texts of The Chartered Insurance Institute, there are the following categories of risk:•Financial risks which means that the risk must have financial measurement.•Pure risks which means that the risk must be real and not related to gambling•Particular risks which means that these risks are not widespread in their effect, for example such as earthquake risk for the region prone to it. It is commonly accepted that only financial, pure and particular risks are insurable.
Price	In ordinary usage, price is the quantity of payment or compensation given by one party to another in return for goods or services. In modern economies, prices are generally expressed in units of some form of currency. (For commodities, they are expressed as currency per unit weight of the commodity, e.g. euros per kilogram).
Health insurance	Health insurance is insurance against the risk of incurring medical expenses among individuals. By estimating the overall risk of health care and health system expenses, among a targeted group, an insurer can develop a routine finance structure, such as a monthly premium or payroll tax, to ensure that money is available to pay for the health care benefits specified in the insurance agreement. The benefit is administered by a central organization such as a government agency, private business, or not-for-profit entity.
Problem	A problem, which can be caused for different reasons, and, if solvable, can usually be solved in a number of different ways, is defined in a number of different ways. This is determined by the context in which a said problems is defined. When discussed, a problem can be argued in multiple ways.

19. Population aging and the future of health policy

End-of-life	'End-of-life' is a term used with respect to a product supplied to customers, indicating that the product is in the end of its useful life (from the vendor's point-of-view), and a vendor intends to stop marketing, selling, or sustaining it. (The vendor may simply intend to limit or end support for the product). In the specific case of product sales, a vendor may employ the more specific term 'end-of-sale' (EOS).
Orphan drug	An orphan drug is a pharmaceutical agent that has been developed specifically to treat a rare medical condition, the condition itself being referred to as an orphan disease. In the US and EU it is easier to gain marketing approval for an orphan drug, and there may be other financial incentives, such as extended exclusivity periods, all intended to encourage the development of drugs which might otherwise lack a sufficient profit motive. The assignment of orphan status to a disease and to any drugs developed to treat it is a matter of public policy in many countries, and has resulted in medical breakthroughs that may not have otherwise been achieved due to the economics of drug research and development.
Tropical disease	Tropical diseases are diseases that are prevalent in or unique to tropical and subtropical regions. The diseases are less prevalent in temperate climates, due in part to the occurrence of a cold season, which controls the insect population by forcing hibernation. Insects such as mosquitoes and flies are by far the most common disease carrier, or vector.
Cuba	Cuba, officially the Republic of Cuba is an island country in the Caribbean. The nation of Cuba comprises the main island of Cuba, the Isla de la Juventud, and several archipelagos. Havana is the capital of Cuba and its largest city.

1. A _____ is any period marked by a greatly increased birth rate. This demographic phenomenon is usually ascribed within certain geographical bounds. People born during such a period are often called baby boomers; however, some experts distinguish between those born during such demographic _____s and those who identify with the overlapping cultural generations.

    a. Baby boom
    b. Battle of Annaberg
    c. Freikorps Lichtschlag
    d. Freikorps Oberland

2. . In the United States, _____ is a national social insurance program, administered by the U.S. federal government since 1966, that guarantees access to health insurance for Americans aged 65 and older who have worked and paid into the system, and younger people with disabilities as well as people with end stage renal disease (_____.gov, 2012) and persons with amyotrophic lateral sclerosis.

19. Population aging and the future of health policy

As a social insurance program, _____ spreads the financial risk associated with illness across society to protect everyone, and thus has a somewhat different social role from for-profit private insurers, which manage their risk portfolio by adjusting their pricing according to perceived risk.

In 2010, _____ provided health insurance to 48 million Americans--40 million people age 65 and older and eight million younger people with disabilities.

a. Bituah Leumi
b. Medicare
c. Children in Scotland
d. Coupon-eligible converter box

3. The _____ was a catastrophic nuclear accident that occurred on 26 April 1986 at the Chernobyl Nuclear Power Plant in Ukraine (then officially the Ukrainian SSR), which was under the direct jurisdiction of the central authorities of the Soviet Union. An explosion and fire released large quantities of radioactive particles into the atmosphere, which spread over much of the western USSR and Europe.

The _____ is the worst nuclear power plant accident in history in terms of cost and resulting deaths, and is one of only two classified as a level 7 event (the maximum classification) on the International Nuclear Event Scale (the other being the Fukushima Daiichi nuclear disaster in 2011).

a. 1922 confiscation of Russian Orthodox Church property
b. Chernobyl disaster
c. Basis Nord
d. Centrosibir

4. A _____ is a type of small deliberative assembly that is usually intended to remain subordinate to another, larger deliberative assembly--which when organized so that action on _____ requires a vote by all its entitled members, is called the '_____ of the Whole'. _____s often serve several different functions:•Governance: in organizations considered too large for all the members to participate in decisions affecting the organization as a whole, a _____ is given the power to make decisions, spend money, or take actions. Some or all such powers may be limited or effectively unlimited.

a. Committee
b. Fuel protests in the United Kingdom
c. Battle of Annaberg
d. Freikorps Lichtschlag

5. . _____, also known as under-5 mortality, refers to the death of infants and children under the age of five. In 2012, 6.6 million, 2011, 6.9 million children under five died, down from 7.6 million in 2010, 8.1 million in 2009, and 12.4 million in 1990. About half of child deaths occur in Sub-Saharan Africa. Reduction of _____ is the fourth of the United Nations' Millennium Development Goals.

_____ Rate is the highest in low-income countries, such as most countries in Sub-Saharan Africa. A child's death is emotionally and physically damaging for the mourning parents.

a. 1918 flu pandemic
b. CAB Direct
c. Child mortality
d. Child Family Health International

1. a

2. b

3. b

4. a

5. c

You can take the complete Online Interactive Chapter Practice Test

for 19. Population aging and the future of health policy
on all key terms, persons, places, and concepts.

No Additional Costs

http://www.Cram101.com

Register, send an email request to Travis.Reese@Cram101.com to get your user Id and password.

Include your customer order number, and ISBN number from your studyguide Retailer.

20. The economics of health externalities

CHAPTER OUTLINE: KEY TERMS, PEOPLE, PLACES, CONCEPTS

	Budget
	Public health
	Coase theorem
	Welfare
	Demand
	Demand curve
	Price
	Rationing
	Medicaid
	Medicare
	CARE
	Managed care
	Market

20. The economics of health externalities

Budget	A budget is a quantitative expression of a plan for a defined period of time. It may include planned sales volumes and revenues, resource quantities, costs and expenses, assets, liabilities and cash flows. It expresses strategic plans of business units, organizations, activities or events in measurable terms.
Public health	Public health is 'the science and art of preventing disease, prolonging life and promoting health through the organized efforts and informed choices of society, organizations, public and private, communities and individuals.' It is concerned with threats to health based on population health analysis. The population in question can be as small as a handful of people, or as large as all the inhabitants of several continents (for instance, in the case of a pandemic). The dimensions of health can encompass 'a state of complete physical, mental and social well-being and not merely the absence of disease or infirmity', as defined by the United Nations' World Health Organization.
Coase theorem	In law and economics, the Coase theorem describes the economic efficiency of an economic allocation or outcome in the presence of externalities. The theorem states that if trade in an externality is possible and there are sufficiently low transaction costs, bargaining will lead to an efficient outcome regardless of the initial allocation of property. In practice, obstacles to bargaining or poorly defined property rights can prevent Coasian bargaining.
Welfare	Welfare is the provision of a minimal level of well-being and social support for all citizens, sometimes referred to as public aid. In most developed countries welfare is largely provided by the government, and to a lesser extent, charities, informal social groups, religious groups, and inter-governmental organizations.

The welfare state expands on this concept to include services such as universal healthcare and unemployment insurance. |
Demand	In economics, demand for a good or service is an entire listing of the quantity of the good or service that a market would choose to buy, for every possible market price of the good or service. (Note: This distinguishes 'demand' from 'quantity demanded', where demand is a listing or graphing of quantity demanded at each possible price. In contrast to demand, quantity demanded is the exact quantity demanded at a certain price.
Demand curve	In economics, the demand curve is the graph depicting the relationship between the price of a certain commodity and the amount of it that consumers are willing and able to purchase at that given price. It is a graphic representation of a demand schedule. The demand curve for all consumers together follows from the demand curve of every individual consumer: the individual demands at each price are added together.
Price	In ordinary usage, price is the quantity of payment or compensation given by one party to another in return for goods or services.

	In modern economies, prices are generally expressed in units of some form of currency. (For commodities, they are expressed as currency per unit weight of the commodity, e.g. euros per kilogram).
Rationing	Rationing is the controlled distribution of scarce resources, goods, or services. Rationing controls the size of the ration, one's allotted portion of the resources being distributed on a particular day or at a particular time.
Medicaid	Medicaid in the United States is a social health care program for families and individuals with low income and resources. The Health Insurance Association of America describes Medicaid as a 'government insurance program for persons of all ages whose income and resources are insufficient to pay for health care.' (America's Health Insurance Plans (HIAA), pg. 232). Medicaid is the largest source of funding for medical and health-related services for people with low income in the United States.
Medicare	In the United States, Medicare is a national social insurance program, administered by the U.S. federal government since 1966, that guarantees access to health insurance for Americans aged 65 and older who have worked and paid into the system, and younger people with disabilities as well as people with end stage renal disease (Medicare.gov, 2012) and persons with amyotrophic lateral sclerosis. As a social insurance program, Medicare spreads the financial risk associated with illness across society to protect everyone, and thus has a somewhat different social role from for-profit private insurers, which manage their risk portfolio by adjusting their pricing according to perceived risk. In 2010, Medicare provided health insurance to 48 million Americans--40 million people age 65 and older and eight million younger people with disabilities.
CARE	CARE is a major international humanitarian agency delivering broad-spectrum emergency relief and long-term international development projects. Founded in 1945, CARE is nonsectarian, non-partisan, and non-governmental. It is one of the largest and oldest humanitarian aid organizations focused on fighting global poverty.
Managed care	The term managed care or managed health care is used in the United States to describe a variety of techniques intended to reduce the cost of providing health benefits and improve the quality of care ('managed care techniques'), for organizations that use those techniques or provide them as services to other organizations ('managed care organization' or 'MCO'), or to describe systems of financing and delivering health care to enrollees organized around managed care techniques and concepts ('managed care delivery systems').

20. The economics of health externalities

	...intended to reduce unnecessary health care costs through a variety of mechanisms, including: economic incentives for physicians and patients to select less costly forms of care; programs for reviewing the medical necessity of specific services; increased beneficiary cost sharing; controls on inpatient admissions and lengths of stay; the establishment of cost-sharing incentives for outpatient surgery; selective contracting with health care providers; and the intensive management of high-cost health care cases. The programs may be provided in a variety of settings, such as Health Maintenance Organizations and Preferred Provider Organizations.
Market	A market is one of the many varieties of systems, institutions, procedures, social relations and infrastructures whereby parties engage in exchange. While parties may exchange goods and services by barter, most markets rely on sellers offering their goods or services (including labor) in exchange for money from buyers. It can be said that a market is the process by which the prices of goods and services are established.

1. In the United States, _____ is a national social insurance program, administered by the U.S. federal government since 1966, that guarantees access to health insurance for Americans aged 65 and older who have worked and paid into the system, and younger people with disabilities as well as people with end stage renal disease (_____.gov, 2012) and persons with amyotrophic lateral sclerosis. As a social insurance program, _____ spreads the financial risk associated with illness across society to protect everyone, and thus has a somewhat different social role from for-profit private insurers, which manage their risk portfolio by adjusting their pricing according to perceived risk.

    In 2010, _____ provided health insurance to 48 million Americans--40 million people age 65 and older and eight million younger people with disabilities.

    a. Bituah Leumi
    b. Child protection
    c. Children in Scotland
    d. Medicare

2. . In economics, the _____ is the graph depicting the relationship between the price of a certain commodity and the amount of it that consumers are willing and able to purchase at that given price. It is a graphic representation of a demand schedule. The _____ for all consumers together follows from the _____ of every individual consumer: the individual demands at each price are added together.

    a. Beveridge curve

b. Budget constraint

c. Cost curve

d. Demand curve

3. _____ is 'the science and art of preventing disease, prolonging life and promoting health through the organized efforts and informed choices of society, organizations, public and private, communities and individuals.' It is concerned with threats to health based on population health analysis. The population in question can be as small as a handful of people, or as large as all the inhabitants of several continents (for instance, in the case of a pandemic). The dimensions of health can encompass 'a state of complete physical, mental and social well-being and not merely the absence of disease or infirmity', as defined by the United Nations' World Health Organization.

a. Public health

b. Capitation

c. Case mix group

d. Centre for Reviews and Dissemination

4. A _____ is one of the many varieties of systems, institutions, procedures, social relations and infrastructures whereby parties engage in exchange. While parties may exchange goods and services by barter, most _____s rely on sellers offering their goods or services (including labor) in exchange for money from buyers. It can be said that a _____ is the process by which the prices of goods and services are established.

a. Market

b. Fuel protests in the United Kingdom

c. Battle of Annaberg

d. Freikorps Lichtschlag

5. A _____ is a quantitative expression of a plan for a defined period of time. It may include planned sales volumes and revenues, resource quantities, costs and expenses, assets, liabilities and cash flows. It expresses strategic plans of business units, organizations, activities or events in measurable terms.

a. Rachel Ashwell

b. Fuel protests in the United Kingdom

c. Battle of Annaberg

d. Budget

1. d
2. d
3. a
4. a
5. d

You can take the complete Online Interactive Chapter Practice Test

for 20. The economics of health externalities
on all key terms, persons, places, and concepts.

No Additional Costs

http://www.Cram101.com

Register, send an email request to Travis.Reese@Cram101.com to get your user Id and password.

Include your customer order number, and ISBN number from your studyguide Retailer.

21. Economic epidemiology

	Demand
	Screening
	Medicare
	Trust
	Elasticity
	Epidemic
	Prescription
	Control
	Economics
	Welfare
	Welfare economics

CHAPTER HIGHLIGHTS & NOTES: KEY TERMS, PEOPLE, PLACES, CONCEPTS

Demand

In economics, demand for a good or service is an entire listing of the quantity of the good or service that a market would choose to buy, for every possible market price of the good or service. (Note: This distinguishes 'demand' from 'quantity demanded', where demand is a listing or graphing of quantity demanded at each possible price. In contrast to demand, quantity demanded is the exact quantity demanded at a certain price.

Screening

Screening in economics refers to a strategy of combating adverse selection, one of the potential decision-making complications in cases of asymmetric information. The concept of screening was first developed by Michael Spence (1973), and should be distinguished from signalling, which implies that the informed agent moves first.

21. Economic epidemiology

Medicare	In the United States, Medicare is a national social insurance program, administered by the U.S. federal government since 1966, that guarantees access to health insurance for Americans aged 65 and older who have worked and paid into the system, and younger people with disabilities as well as people with end stage renal disease (Medicare.gov, 2012) and persons with amyotrophic lateral sclerosis. As a social insurance program, Medicare spreads the financial risk associated with illness across society to protect everyone, and thus has a somewhat different social role from for-profit private insurers, which manage their risk portfolio by adjusting their pricing according to perceived risk. In 2010, Medicare provided health insurance to 48 million Americans--40 million people age 65 and older and eight million younger people with disabilities.
Trust	A 'trust,' or 'corporate trust' means a large business. Originally, it was Standard Oil, which was already the largest corporation in the world
Elasticity	In economics, elasticity is the measurement of how responsive an economic variable is to a change in another. For example:•'If I lower the price of my product, how much more will I sell?'•'If I raise the price of one good, how will that affect sales of this other good?'•'If we learn that a resource is becoming scarce, will people scramble to acquire it?' An elastic variable (or elasticity value greater than 1) is one which responds more than proportionally to changes in other variables. In contrast, an inelastic variable (or elasticity value less than 1) is one which changes less than proportionally in response to changes in other variables.
Epidemic	In epidemiology, an epidemic occurs when new cases of a certain disease, in a given human population, and during a given period, substantially exceed what is expected based on recent experience. Epidemiologists often consider the term outbreak to be synonymous to epidemic, but the general public typically perceives outbreaks to be more local and less serious than epidemics. Epidemics of infectious disease are generally caused by a change in the ecology of the host population (e.g. increased stress or increase in the density of a vector species), a genetic change in the parasite population or the introduction of a new parasite to a host population (by movement of parasites or hosts).
Prescription	In law, prescription is the method of sovereignty transfer of a territory through international law analogous to the common law doctrine of adverse possession for private real-estate. Prescription involves the open encroachment by the new sovereign upon the territory in question for a prolonged period of time, acting as the sovereign, without protest or other contest by the original sovereign. This doctrine legalizes de jure the de facto transfer of sovereignty caused in part by the original sovereign's extended negligence and/or neglect of the area in question.

21. Economic epidemiology

Control	Controlling is one of the managerial functions like planning, organizing, staffing and directing. It is an important function because it helps to check the errors and to take the corrective action so that deviation from standards are minimized and stated goals of the organization are achieved in a desired manner. According to modern concepts, control is a foreseeing action whereas earlier concept of control was used only when errors were detected.
Economics	Economics is the social science that studies the behavior of individuals, households, and organizations, when they manage or use scarce resources, which have alternative uses, to achieve desired ends. Agents are assumed to act rationally, have multiple desirable ends in sight, limited resources to obtain these ends, a set of stable preferences, a definite overall guiding objective, and the capability of making a choice. There exists an economic problem, subject to study by economic science, when a decision (choice) has to be made by one or more resource-controlling players to attain the best possible outcome under bounded rational conditions.
Welfare	Welfare is the provision of a minimal level of well-being and social support for all citizens, sometimes referred to as public aid. In most developed countries welfare is largely provided by the government, and to a lesser extent, charities, informal social groups, religious groups, and inter-governmental organizations. The welfare state expands on this concept to include services such as universal healthcare and unemployment insurance.
Welfare economics	Welfare economics is a branch of economics that uses microeconomic techniques to evaluate well-being from allocation of productive factors as to desirability and economic efficiency within an economy, often relative to competitive general equilibrium. It analyzes social welfare, however measured, in terms of economic activities of the individuals that compose the theoretical society considered. Accordingly, individuals, with associated economic activities, are the basic units for aggregating to social welfare, whether of a group, a community, or a society, and there is no 'social welfare' apart from the 'welfare' associated with its individual units.

21. Economic epidemiology

1. _____ in economics refers to a strategy of combating adverse selection, one of the potential decision-making complications in cases of asymmetric information. The concept of _____ was first developed by Michael Spence (1973), and should be distinguished from signalling, which implies that the informed agent moves first.

    For purposes of _____, asymmetric information cases assume two economic agents--which we call, for example, Abel and Cain--where Abel knows more about himself than Cain knows about Abel.

    a. Capitation fee
    b. Deskilling
    c. Higher education bubble
    d. Screening

2. In economics, _____ for a good or service is an entire listing of the quantity of the good or service that a market would choose to buy, for every possible market price of the good or service. (Note: This distinguishes '_____' from 'quantity demanded', where _____ is a listing or graphing of quantity demanded at each possible price. In contrast to _____, quantity demanded is the exact quantity demanded at a certain price.

    a. Budget set
    b. Complementary good
    c. Consumer service
    d. Demand

3. A '_____,' or 'corporate _____' means a large business. Originally, it was Standard Oil, which was already the largest corporation in the world

    a. Barriers to exit
    b. Bilateral monopoly
    c. Building block model
    d. Trust

4. _____ is the social science that studies the behavior of individuals, households, and organizations, when they manage or use scarce resources, which have alternative uses, to achieve desired ends. Agents are assumed to act rationally, have multiple desirable ends in sight, limited resources to obtain these ends, a set of stable preferences, a definite overall guiding objective, and the capability of making a choice. There exists an _____(s) problem, subject to study by _____(s) science, when a decision (choice) has to be made by one or more resource-controlling players to attain the best possible outcome under bounded rational conditions.

    a. Economics
    b. Swedish Academy
    c. Molson
    d. Boston Stock Exchange

5. . In economics, _____ is the measurement of how responsive an economic variable is to a change in another.

21. Economic epidemiology

For example:•'If I lower the price of my product, how much more will I sell?'•'If I raise the price of one good, how will that affect sales of this other good?'•'If we learn that a resource is becoming scarce, will people scramble to acquire it?'

An elastic variable (or _____ value greater than 1) is one which responds more than proportionally to changes in other variables. In contrast, an inelastic variable (or _____ value less than 1) is one which changes less than proportionally in response to changes in other variables.

a. Benefit principle
b. Bliss point
c. Club good
d. Elasticity

1. d
2. d
3. d
4. a
5. d

You can take the complete Online Interactive Chapter Practice Test

for 21. Economic epidemiology
on all key terms, persons, places, and concepts.

No Additional Costs

http://www.Cram101.com

Register, send an email request to Travis.Reese@Cram101.com to get your user Id and password.

Include your customer order number, and ISBN number from your studyguide Retailer.

22. Obesity

CHAPTER OUTLINE: KEY TERMS, PEOPLE, PLACES, CONCEPTS

	Cuba
	Index
	Food industry
	Price
	Trends
	Labor force
	Participation
	Welfare
	Committee
	Good
	Thing
	Crisis
	Health crisis
	Public health
	Health insurance
	Insurance
	Moral hazard
	Budget
	Intervention
	Chernobyl disaster
	Utility

22. Obesity

	Behavioral economics
	Economics

Cuba	Cuba, officially the Republic of Cuba is an island country in the Caribbean. The nation of Cuba comprises the main island of Cuba, the Isla de la Juventud, and several archipelagos. Havana is the capital of Cuba and its largest city.
Index	In economics and finance, an index is a statistical measure of changes in a representative group of individual data points. These data may be derived from any number of sources, including company performance, prices, productivity, and employment. Economic indices (index, plural) track economic health from different perspectives.
Food industry	The food industry is a complex, global collective of diverse businesses that supply much of the food energy consumed by the world population. Only subsistence farmers, those who survive on what they grow, can be considered outside of the scope of the modern food industry. The food industry includes:•Regulation: local, regional, national and international rules and regulations for food production and sale, including food quality and food safety, and industry lobbying activities•Education: academic, vocational, consultancy•Research and development: food technology•Financial services insurance, credit•Manufacturing: agrichemicals, seed, farm machinery and supplies, agricultural construction, etc.•Agriculture: raising of crops and livestock, seafood•Food processing: preparation of fresh products for market, manufacture of prepared food products•Marketing: promotion of generic products (e.g. milk board), new products, public opinion, through advertising, packaging, public relations, et•Wholesale and distribution: warehousing, transportation, logistics•Retailing
Price	In ordinary usage, price is the quantity of payment or compensation given by one party to another in return for goods or services. In modern economies, prices are generally expressed in units of some form of currency. (For commodities, they are expressed as currency per unit weight of the commodity, e.g. euros per kilogram).
Trends	Trends is a society, philanthropy, fashion and lifestyle magazine published in Arizona.

	Created by Danny Medina in 1982, it was purchased by Bill Dougherty in 2001, who now serves as its publisher.
	Trends has a 501(c)(3) arm, the Trends Charitable Fund (TCF), which raises money for underserved women's and children's charitable organizations.
Labor force	The labor force is the actual number of people available for work. The labor force of a country includes both the employed and the unemployed. The labor force participation rate, LFPR (or economic activity rate, EAR), is the ratio between the labor force and the overall size of their cohort (national population of the same age range).
Participation	In finance, 'participation' is an ownership interest in a mortgage or other loan. In particular, loan participation is a cooperation of multiple lenders to issue a loan (known as participation loan) to one borrower. This is usually done in order to reduce individual risks of the lenders.
Welfare	Welfare is the provision of a minimal level of well-being and social support for all citizens, sometimes referred to as public aid. In most developed countries welfare is largely provided by the government, and to a lesser extent, charities, informal social groups, religious groups, and inter-governmental organizations. The welfare state expands on this concept to include services such as universal healthcare and unemployment insurance.
Committee	A committee is a type of small deliberative assembly that is usually intended to remain subordinate to another, larger deliberative assembly--which when organized so that action on committee requires a vote by all its entitled members, is called the 'Committee of the Whole'. Committees often serve several different functions:•Governance: in organizations considered too large for all the members to participate in decisions affecting the organization as a whole, a committee is given the power to make decisions, spend money, or take actions. Some or all such powers may be limited or effectively unlimited.
Good	In economics, a good is a material that satisfies human wants and provides utility, for example, to a consumer making a purchase. A common distinction is made between 'goods' that are tangible property (also called goods) and services, which are non-physical. Commodities may be used as a synonym for economic goods but often refer to marketable raw materials and primary products.
Thing	The Thing, also known as the Great Seal bug, was one of the first covert listening devices to use passive techniques to transmit an audio signal. Because it was passive, being energized and activated by electromagnetic energy from an outside source, it is considered a predecessor of current RFID technology.

22. Obesity

Crisis	A crisis is any event that is, or is expected to lead to, an unstable and dangerous situation affecting an individual, group, community, or whole society. Crises are deemed to be negative changes in the security, economic, political, societal, or environmental affairs, especially when they occur abruptly, with little or no warning. More loosely, it is a term meaning 'a testing time' or an 'emergency event'.
Health crisis	A health crisis or public health crisis is a difficult situation or complex health system that affects humans in one or more geographic areas, from a particular locality to encompass the entire planet. Health crises generally have significant impacts on community health, loss of life, and on the economy. They may result from disease, industrial processes or poor policy.
Public health	Public health is 'the science and art of preventing disease, prolonging life and promoting health through the organized efforts and informed choices of society, organizations, public and private, communities and individuals.' It is concerned with threats to health based on population health analysis. The population in question can be as small as a handful of people, or as large as all the inhabitants of several continents (for instance, in the case of a pandemic). The dimensions of health can encompass 'a state of complete physical, mental and social well-being and not merely the absence of disease or infirmity', as defined by the United Nations' World Health Organization.
Health insurance	Health insurance is insurance against the risk of incurring medical expenses among individuals. By estimating the overall risk of health care and health system expenses, among a targeted group, an insurer can develop a routine finance structure, such as a monthly premium or payroll tax, to ensure that money is available to pay for the health care benefits specified in the insurance agreement. The benefit is administered by a central organization such as a government agency, private business, or not-for-profit entity.
Insurance	Insurance is the equitable transfer of the risk of a loss, from one entity to another in exchange for payment. It is a form of risk management primarily used to hedge against the risk of a contingent, uncertain loss.
	According to study texts of The Chartered Insurance Institute, there are the following categories of risk:•Financial risks which means that the risk must have financial measurement.•Pure risks which means that the risk must be real and not related to gambling•Particular risks which means that these risks are not widespread in their effect, for example such as earthquake risk for the region prone to it.
	It is commonly accepted that only financial, pure and particular risks are insurable.
Moral hazard	In economic theory, a moral hazard is a situation where a party will have a tendency to take risks because the costs that could result will not be felt by the party taking the risk. In other words, it is a tendency to be more willing to take a risk, knowing that the potential costs or burdens of taking such risk will be borne, in whole or in part, by others.

Budget	A budget is a quantitative expression of a plan for a defined period of time. It may include planned sales volumes and revenues, resource quantities, costs and expenses, assets, liabilities and cash flows. It expresses strategic plans of business units, organizations, activities or events in measurable terms.
Intervention	Intervention, in terms of international law, is the term for the use of force by one country or sovereign state in the internal or external affairs of another. In most cases, intervention is considered to be an unlawfu. l
Chernobyl disaster	The Chernobyl disaster was a catastrophic nuclear accident that occurred on 26 April 1986 at the Chernobyl Nuclear Power Plant in Ukraine (then officially the Ukrainian SSR), which was under the direct jurisdiction of the central authorities of the Soviet Union. An explosion and fire released large quantities of radioactive particles into the atmosphere, which spread over much of the western USSR and Europe. The Chernobyl disaster is the worst nuclear power plant accident in history in terms of cost and resulting deaths, and is one of only two classified as a level 7 event (the maximum classification) on the International Nuclear Event Scale (the other being the Fukushima Daiichi nuclear disaster in 2011).
Utility	Utility, or usefulness, is the ability of something to satisfy needs or wants. Utility is an important concept in economics and game theory, because it represents satisfaction experienced by the consumer of a good. Not coincidentally, a good is something that satisfies human wants and provides utility, for example, to a consumer making a purchase.
Behavioral economics	Behavioral economics and the related field, behavioral finance, study the effects of social, cognitive, and emotional factors on the economic decisions of individuals and institutions and the consequences for market prices, returns, and the resource allocation. The fields are primarily concerned with the bounds of rationality of economic agents. Behavioral models typically integrate insights from psychology with microeconomic theory; in so doing, these behavioral models cover a range of concepts, methods, and fields.
Economics	Economics is the social science that studies the behavior of individuals, households, and organizations, when they manage or use scarce resources, which have alternative uses, to achieve desired ends. Agents are assumed to act rationally, have multiple desirable ends in sight, limited resources to obtain these ends, a set of stable preferences, a definite overall guiding objective, and the capability of making a choice. There exists an economic problem, subject to study by economic science, when a decision (choice) has to be made by one or more resource-controlling players to attain the best possible outcome under bounded rational conditions.

22. Obesity

1. The _____ is a complex, global collective of diverse businesses that supply much of the food energy consumed by the world population. Only subsistence farmers, those who survive on what they grow, can be considered outside of the scope of the modern _____.

   The _____ includes:•Regulation: local, regional, national and international rules and regulations for food production and sale, including food quality and food safety, and industry lobbying activities•Education: academic, vocational, consultancy•Research and development: food technology•Financial services insurance, credit•Manufacturing: agrichemicals, seed, farm machinery and supplies, agricultural construction, etc.•Agriculture: raising of crops and livestock, seafood•Food processing: preparation of fresh products for market, manufacture of prepared food products•Marketing: promotion of generic products (e.g. milk board), new products, public opinion, through advertising, packaging, public relations, et•Wholesale and distribution: warehousing, transportation, logistics•Retailing

   a. Fuel protests in the United Kingdom
   b. Food industry
   c. Freikorps Lichtschlag
   d. Freikorps Oberland

2. The _____, also known as the Great Seal bug, was one of the first covert listening devices to use passive techniques to transmit an audio signal. Because it was passive, being energized and activated by electromagnetic energy from an outside source, it is considered a predecessor of current RFID technology.

   a. 1801 series CPU
   b. Thing
   c. Berkovich tip
   d. BESM

3. _____, officially the Republic of _____ is an island country in the Caribbean. The nation of _____ comprises the main island of _____, the Isla de la Juventud, and several archipelagos. Havana is the capital of _____ and its largest city.

   a. Central Asian-American Enterprise Fund
   b. China
   c. Cuba
   d. Fuel protests in the United Kingdom

4. . A _____ is a type of small deliberative assembly that is usually intended to remain subordinate to another, larger deliberative assembly--which when organized so that action on _____ requires a vote by all its entitled members, is called the '_____ of the Whole'. _____s often serve several different functions:•Governance: in organizations considered too large for all the members to participate in decisions affecting the organization as a whole, a _____ is given the power to make decisions, spend money, or take actions. Some or all such powers may be limited or effectively unlimited.

   a. Chloroform Committee

b. Fuel protests in the United Kingdom

c. Committee

d. Freikorps Lichtschlag

5. _____, in terms of international law, is the term for the use of force by one country or sovereign state in the internal or external affairs of another. In most cases, _____ is considered to be an unlawfu. l

a. Bombardier Aerospace and Embraer S.A. government subsidy controversy

b. Intervention

c. Caroline test

d. Central Authority

1. b
2. b
3. c
4. c
5. b

You can take the complete Online Interactive Chapter Practice Test

for 22. Obesity
on all key terms, persons, places, and concepts.

No Additional Costs

http://www.Cram101.com

Register, send an email request to Travis.Reese@Cram101.com to get your user Id and password.

Include your customer order number, and ISBN number from your studyguide Retailer.

23. Prospect theory

CHAPTER OUTLINE: KEY TERMS, PEOPLE, PLACES, CONCEPTS

Prospect theory

Theory

Behavioral economics

Economics

Health insurance

Insurance

Utility

Price

Rationing

Loss aversion

Point

Index

Evaluation

Value

CARE

Demand

Intervention

Budget

Cost-effectiveness analysis

Health technology assessment

Technology assessment

23. Prospect theory

Prospect theory	Prospect theory is a behavioral economic theory that describes the way people choose between probabilistic alternatives that involve risk, where the probabilities of outcomes are known. The theory states that people make decisions based on the potential value of losses and gains rather than the final outcome, and that people evaluate these losses and gains using certain heuristics. The model is descriptive: it tries to model real-life choices, rather than optimal decisions.
Theory	Theory is a group of ideas meant to explain a certain topic of science, such as a single or collection of fact, event(s), or phenomen(a)(on). Typically, a theory is developed through the use of contemplative and rational forms of abstract and generalized thinking. Furthermore, a theory is often based on general principles that are independent of the thing being explained.
Behavioral economics	Behavioral economics and the related field, behavioral finance, study the effects of social, cognitive, and emotional factors on the economic decisions of individuals and institutions and the consequences for market prices, returns, and the resource allocation. The fields are primarily concerned with the bounds of rationality of economic agents. Behavioral models typically integrate insights from psychology with microeconomic theory; in so doing, these behavioral models cover a range of concepts, methods, and fields.
Economics	Economics is the social science that studies the behavior of individuals, households, and organizations, when they manage or use scarce resources, which have alternative uses, to achieve desired ends. Agents are assumed to act rationally, have multiple desirable ends in sight, limited resources to obtain these ends, a set of stable preferences, a definite overall guiding objective, and the capability of making a choice. There exists an economic problem, subject to study by economic science, when a decision (choice) has to be made by one or more resource-controlling players to attain the best possible outcome under bounded rational conditions.
Health insurance	Health insurance is insurance against the risk of incurring medical expenses among individuals. By estimating the overall risk of health care and health system expenses, among a targeted group, an insurer can develop a routine finance structure, such as a monthly premium or payroll tax, to ensure that money is available to pay for the health care benefits specified in the insurance agreement. The benefit is administered by a central organization such as a government agency, private business, or not-for-profit entity.
Insurance	Insurance is the equitable transfer of the risk of a loss, from one entity to another in exchange for payment. It is a form of risk management primarily used to hedge against the risk of a contingent, uncertain loss. According to study texts of The Chartered Insurance Institute, there are the following categories of risk:•Financial risks which means that the risk must have financial measurement.•Pure risks which means that the risk must be real and not related to gambling•Particular risks which means that these risks are not widespread in their effect, for example such as earthquake risk for the region prone to it.

Utility	Utility, or usefulness, is the ability of something to satisfy needs or wants. Utility is an important concept in economics and game theory, because it represents satisfaction experienced by the consumer of a good. Not coincidentally, a good is something that satisfies human wants and provides utility, for example, to a consumer making a purchase.
Price	In ordinary usage, price is the quantity of payment or compensation given by one party to another in return for goods or services. In modern economies, prices are generally expressed in units of some form of currency. (For commodities, they are expressed as currency per unit weight of the commodity, e.g. euros per kilogram).
Rationing	Rationing is the controlled distribution of scarce resources, goods, or services. Rationing controls the size of the ration, one's allotted portion of the resources being distributed on a particular day or at a particular time.
Loss aversion	In economics and decision theory, loss aversion refers to people's tendency to strongly prefer avoiding losses to acquiring gains. Some studies suggest that losses are twice as powerful, psychologically, as gains. Loss aversion was first demonstrated by Amos Tversky and Daniel Kahneman.
Point	Points, sometimes also called 'discount points', are a form of pre-paid interest. One point equals one percent of the loan amount. By charging a borrower points, a lender effectively increases the yield on the loan above the amount of the stated interest rate.
Index	In economics and finance, an index is a statistical measure of changes in a representative group of individual data points. These data may be derived from any number of sources, including company performance, prices, productivity, and employment. Economic indices (index, plural) track economic health from different perspectives.
Evaluation	In the workplace, an evaluation is a tool employers use to review the performance of an employee. Usually, the employee's supervisor is responsible for evaluating the employee. A private conference is often scheduled to discuss the evaluation.
Value	Economic value is a measure of the benefit that an economic actor can gain from either a good or service. It is generally measured relative to units of currency, and the interpretation is therefore 'what is the maximum amount of money a specific actor is willing and able to pay for the good or service'? Note that economic value is not the same as market price. If a consumer is willing to buy a good, it implies that the customer places a higher value on the good than the market price.

23. Prospect theory

CARE	CARE is a major international humanitarian agency delivering broad-spectrum emergency relief and long-term international development projects. Founded in 1945, CARE is nonsectarian, non-partisan, and non-governmental. It is one of the largest and oldest humanitarian aid organizations focused on fighting global poverty.
Demand	In economics, demand for a good or service is an entire listing of the quantity of the good or service that a market would choose to buy, for every possible market price of the good or service. (Note: This distinguishes 'demand' from 'quantity demanded', where demand is a listing or graphing of quantity demanded at each possible price. In contrast to demand, quantity demanded is the exact quantity demanded at a certain price.
Intervention	Intervention, in terms of international law, is the term for the use of force by one country or sovereign state in the internal or external affairs of another. In most cases, intervention is considered to be an unlawfu. l
Budget	A budget is a quantitative expression of a plan for a defined period of time. It may include planned sales volumes and revenues, resource quantities, costs and expenses, assets, liabilities and cash flows. It expresses strategic plans of business units, organizations, activities or events in measurable terms.
Cost-effectiveness analysis	Cost-effectiveness analysis is a form of economic analysis that compares the relative costs and outcomes (effects) of two or more courses of action. Cost-effectiveness analysis is distinct from cost-benefit analysis, which assigns a monetary value to the measure of effect. Cost-effectiveness analysis is often used in the field of health services, where it may be inappropriate to monetize health effect.
Health technology assessment	Health technology assessment is a multi-disciplinary field of policy analysis that studies the medical, social, ethical, and economic implications of development, diffusion, and use of health technology. It has other definitions including 'the systematic evaluation of the properties and effects of a health technology, addressing the direct and intended effects of this technology, as well as its indirect and unintended consequences, and aimed mainly at informing decision making regarding health technologies.' and 'a multidisciplinary process that summarises information about the medical, social, economic and ethical issues related to the use of a health technology in a systematic, transparent, unbiased, robust manner. Its aim is to inform the formulation of safe, effective, health policies that are patient focused and seek to achieve best value.
Technology assessment	Technology assessment is a scientific, interactive, and communicative process that aims to contribute to the formation of public and political opinion on societal aspects of science and technology.

23. Prospect theory

1. _____ is a multi-disciplinary field of policy analysis that studies the medical, social, ethical, and economic implications of development, diffusion, and use of health technology. It has other definitions including 'the systematic evaluation of the properties and effects of a health technology, addressing the direct and intended effects of this technology, as well as its indirect and unintended consequences, and aimed mainly at informing decision making regarding health technologies.' and 'a multidisciplinary process that summarises information about the medical, social, economic and ethical issues related to the use of a health technology in a systematic, transparent, unbiased, robust manner. Its aim is to inform the formulation of safe, effective, health policies that are patient focused and seek to achieve best value.

   a. 100 Best Workplaces in Europe
   b. Health technology assessment
   c. CESG Claims Tested Mark
   d. Commercial Product Assurance

2. _____ is the controlled distribution of scarce resources, goods, or services. _____ controls the size of the ration, one's allotted portion of the resources being distributed on a particular day or at a particular time.

   a. Fuel protests in the United Kingdom
   b. Bachelor tax
   c. Rationing
   d. Brick tax

3. _____ is the equitable transfer of the risk of a loss, from one entity to another in exchange for payment. It is a form of risk management primarily used to hedge against the risk of a contingent, uncertain loss.

   According to study texts of The Chartered _____ Institute, there are the following categories of risk:•Financial risks which means that the risk must have financial measurement.•Pure risks which means that the risk must be real and not related to gambling•Particular risks which means that these risks are not widespread in their effect, for example such as earthquake risk for the region prone to it.

   It is commonly accepted that only financial, pure and particular risks are insurable.

   a. Fuel protests in the United Kingdom
   b. Insurance
   c. Freikorps Lichtschlag
   d. Freikorps Oberland

4. . _____ is a group of ideas meant to explain a certain topic of science, such as a single or collection of fact, event (s), or phenomen(a)(on). Typically, a _____ is developed through the use of contemplative and rational forms of abstract and generalized thinking. Furthermore, a _____ is often based on general principles that are independent of the thing being explained.

   a. Bayesian probability
   b. Theory

23. Prospect theory

c. Biofact

d. Biological determinism

5. _____ is a behavioral economic theory that describes the way people choose between probabilistic alternatives that involve risk, where the probabilities of outcomes are known. The theory states that people make decisions based on the potential value of losses and gains rather than the final outcome, and that people evaluate these losses and gains using certain heuristics. The model is descriptive: it tries to model real-life choices, rather than optimal decisions.

a. Behavioral clustering

b. Blissful ignorance effect

c. Prospect theory

d. Canadian Index of Consumer Confidence

1. b
2. c
3. b
4. b
5. c

You can take the complete Online Interactive Chapter Practice Test

for 23. Prospect theory
on all key terms, persons, places, and concepts.

No Additional Costs

http://www.Cram101.com

Register, send an email request to Travis.Reese@Cram101.com to get your user Id and password.

Include your customer order number, and ISBN number from your studyguide Retailer.

24. Time inconsistency and health

CHAPTER OUTLINE: KEY TERMS, PEOPLE, PLACES, CONCEPTS

	Discount function
	Price
	Discounting
	Preference
	Health insurance
	Insurance
	Rational addiction
	Demand
	Mechanism
	Cuba
	Gradient
	Retirement
	Saving
	Committee
	Dictatorship
	Economics
	Perspective
	Revealed preference
	Welfare
	Welfare economics
	Intervention

24. Time inconsistency and health

CHAPTER OUTLINE: KEY TERMS, PEOPLE, PLACES, CONCEPTS

	Hypothesis

	Time preference

CHAPTER HIGHLIGHTS & NOTES: KEY TERMS, PEOPLE, PLACES, CONCEPTS

Discount function	A discount function is used in economic models to describe the weights placed on rewards received at different points in time. For example, if time is discrete and utility is time-separable, with the discount function $f(t)$ and with $c(t)$ defined as consumption at time t, total utility is given by $$U(\{c_t\}_{t=0}^{\infty}) = \sum_{t=0}^{\infty} f(t)u(c_t)$$. Total utility in the continuous-time case is given by $$U(\{c(t)\}_{t=0}^{\infty}) = \int_0^{\infty} f(t)u(c(t))dt$$ provided that this integral exists. Exponential discounting and hyperbolic discounting are the two most commonly used examples.
Price	In ordinary usage, price is the quantity of payment or compensation given by one party to another in return for goods or services. In modern economies, prices are generally expressed in units of some form of currency. (For commodities, they are expressed as currency per unit weight of the commodity, e.g. euros per kilogram).
Discounting	Discounting is a financial mechanism in which a debtor obtains the right to delay payments to a creditor, for a defined period of time, in exchange for a charge or fee. Essentially, the party that owes money in the present purchases the right to delay the payment until some future date. The discount, or charge, is the difference (expressed as a difference in the same units (absolute) or in percentage terms (relative), or as a ratio) between the original amount owed in the present and the amount that has to be paid in the future to settle the debt.

Preference	In economics and other social sciences, preference refers to the set of assumptions related to ordering some alternatives, based on the degree of happiness, satisfaction, gratification, enjoyment, or utility they provide, a process which results in an optimal 'choice' . Although economists are usually not interested in choices or preferences in themselves, they are interested in the theory of choice because it serves as a background for empirical demand analysis.
Health insurance	Health insurance is insurance against the risk of incurring medical expenses among individuals. By estimating the overall risk of health care and health system expenses, among a targeted group, an insurer can develop a routine finance structure, such as a monthly premium or payroll tax, to ensure that money is available to pay for the health care benefits specified in the insurance agreement. The benefit is administered by a central organization such as a government agency, private business, or not-for-profit entity.
Insurance	Insurance is the equitable transfer of the risk of a loss, from one entity to another in exchange for payment. It is a form of risk management primarily used to hedge against the risk of a contingent, uncertain loss. According to study texts of The Chartered Insurance Institute, there are the following categories of risk:•Financial risks which means that the risk must have financial measurement.•Pure risks which means that the risk must be real and not related to gambling•Particular risks which means that these risks are not widespread in their effect, for example such as earthquake risk for the region prone to it. It is commonly accepted that only financial, pure and particular risks are insurable.
Rational addiction	Rational addiction is the hypothesis that addictions can be usefully modeled as specific kinds of rational, forward-looking, optimal consumption plans. The canonical theory comes from work done by Kevin M. Murphy and Nobel Laureate Gary S. Becker
Demand	In economics, demand for a good or service is an entire listing of the quantity of the good or service that a market would choose to buy, for every possible market price of the good or service. (Note: This distinguishes 'demand' from 'quantity demanded', where demand is a listing or graphing of quantity demanded at each possible price. In contrast to demand, quantity demanded is the exact quantity demanded at a certain price.
Mechanism	 The term social mechanisms and mechanism-based explanations of social phenomenon originate from the philosophy of science. The core idea behind the mechanism approach has been expressed as follows by Elster : "To explain an event is to give an account of why it happened.

24. Time inconsistency and health

Cuba	Cuba, officially the Republic of Cuba is an island country in the Caribbean. The nation of Cuba comprises the main island of Cuba, the Isla de la Juventud, and several archipelagos. Havana is the capital of Cuba and its largest city.
Gradient	In mathematics, the gradient is a generalization of the usual concept of derivative of a function in one dimension to a function in several dimensions. If $f(x_1, .. x_n)$ is a differentiable, scalar-valued function of standard Cartesian coordinates in Euclidean space, its gradient is the vector whose components are the n partial derivatives of f. It is thus a vector-valued function.
Retirement	Retirement is the point where a person stops employment completely. A person may also semi-retire by reducing work hours. Many people choose to retire when they are eligible for private or public pension benefits, although some are forced to retire when physical conditions no longer allow the person to work any more (by illness or accident) or as a result of legislation concerning their position.
Saving	Saving is income not spent, or deferred consumption. Methods of saving include putting money aside in a bank or pension plan. Saving also includes reducing expenditures, such as recurring costs.
Committee	A committee is a type of small deliberative assembly that is usually intended to remain subordinate to another, larger deliberative assembly--which when organized so that action on committee requires a vote by all its entitled members, is called the 'Committee of the Whole'. Committees often serve several different functions:•Governance: in organizations considered too large for all the members to participate in decisions affecting the organization as a whole, a committee is given the power to make decisions, spend money, or take actions. Some or all such powers may be limited or effectively unlimited.
Dictatorship	Dictatorship is a form of government ruled by a single leader. The political authority is often monopolized by a single person or a political party, and exercised through various oppressive mechanisms. For some scholars, a dictatorship is a form of government that has the power to govern without the consent of those being governed (similar to authoritarianism), while totalitarianism describes a state that regulates nearly every aspect of the public and private behavior of its people.
Economics	Economics is the social science that studies the behavior of individuals, households, and organizations, when they manage or use scarce resources, which have alternative uses, to achieve desired ends. Agents are assumed to act rationally, have multiple desirable ends in sight, limited resources to obtain these ends, a set of stable preferences, a definite overall guiding objective, and the capability of making a choice.

Perspective	Perspective in pharmacoeconomics refers to the economic vantage point of a pharmacoeconomic analysis, such as a cost-effectiveness analysis or cost-utility analysis. This affects the types of costs (resource expenditures) and benefits that are relevant to the analysis. Five general perspectives are often cited in pharmacoeconomics, including institutional, third party, patient, governmental and societal.
Revealed preference	Revealed preference theory, pioneered by American economist Paul Samuelson, is a method of analyzing choices made by individuals, mostly used for comparing the influence of policies on consumer behavior. These models assume that the preferences of consumers can be revealed by their purchasing habits. Revealed preference theory came about because existing theories of consumer demand were based on a diminishing marginal rate of substitution (MRS).
Welfare	Welfare is the provision of a minimal level of well-being and social support for all citizens, sometimes referred to as public aid. In most developed countries welfare is largely provided by the government, and to a lesser extent, charities, informal social groups, religious groups, and inter-governmental organizations. The welfare state expands on this concept to include services such as universal healthcare and unemployment insurance.
Welfare economics	Welfare economics is a branch of economics that uses microeconomic techniques to evaluate well-being from allocation of productive factors as to desirability and economic efficiency within an economy, often relative to competitive general equilibrium. It analyzes social welfare, however measured, in terms of economic activities of the individuals that compose the theoretical society considered. Accordingly, individuals, with associated economic activities, are the basic units for aggregating to social welfare, whether of a group, a community, or a society, and there is no 'social welfare' apart from the 'welfare' associated with its individual units.
Intervention	Intervention, in terms of international law, is the term for the use of force by one country or sovereign state in the internal or external affairs of another. In most cases, intervention is considered to be an unlawfu. l
Hypothesis	A hypothesis is a proposed explanation for a phenomenon. For a hypothesis to be a scientific hypothesis, the scientific method requires that one can test it. Scientists generally base scientific hypotheses on previous observations that cannot satisfactorily be explained with the available scientific theories.
Time preference	In economics, time preference is the relative valuation placed on a good at an earlier date compared with its valuation at a later date.

24. Time inconsistency and health

There is no absolute distinction that separates 'high' and 'low' time preference, only comparisons with others either individually or in aggregate. Someone with a high time preference is focused substantially on his well-being in the present and the immediate future relative to the average person, while someone with low time preference places more emphasis than average on their well-being in the further future.

1. A _____ is used in economic models to describe the weights placed on rewards received at different points in time. For example, if time is discrete and utility is time-separable, with the _____ $f(t)$ and with $c(t)$ defined as consumption at time t,

   total utility is given by
   $$U(\{c_t\}_{t=0}^{\infty}) = \sum_{t=0}^{\infty} f(t)u(c_t)$$
   .

   Total utility in the continuous-time case is given by $U(\{c(t)\}_{t=0}^{\infty}) = \int_{0}^{\infty} f(t)u(c(t))dt$

   provided that this integral exists.

   Exponential discounting and hyperbolic discounting are the two most commonly used examples.

   a. Fuel protests in the United Kingdom
   b. Battle of Annaberg
   c. Freikorps Lichtschlag
   d. Discount function

2. . _____ theory, pioneered by American economist Paul Samuelson, is a method of analyzing choices made by individuals, mostly used for comparing the influence of policies on consumer behavior. These models assume that the preferences of consumers can be revealed by their purchasing habits. _____ theory came about because existing theories of consumer demand were based on a diminishing marginal rate of substitution (MRS).

   a. Revealed preference
   b. Complementary good
   c. Consumer service

3. _____ is the point where a person stops employment completely. A person may also semi-retire by reducing work hours.

Many people choose to retire when they are eligible for private or public pension benefits, although some are forced to retire when physical conditions no longer allow the person to work any more (by illness or accident) or as a result of legislation concerning their position.

a. Banishment room
b. Constructive dismissal
c. Retirement
d. Letter of resignation

4. _____ is a form of government ruled by a single leader. The political authority is often monopolized by a single person or a political party, and exercised through various oppressive mechanisms.

For some scholars, a _____ is a form of government that has the power to govern without the consent of those being governed (similar to authoritarianism), while totalitarianism describes a state that regulates nearly every aspect of the public and private behavior of its people.

a. Dictator
b. Fuel protests in the United Kingdom
c. Battle of Annaberg
d. Dictatorship

5.

The term social _____s and _____-based explanations of social phenomenon originate from the philosophy of science.

The core idea behind the _____ approach has been expressed as follows by Elster : "To explain an event is to give an account of why it happened. Usually... this takes the form of citing an earlier event as the cause of the event we want to explain....

a. Bayesian probability
b. Berlin Circle
c. Biofact
d. Mechanism

ANSWER KEY
24. Time inconsistency and health

1. d
2. a
3. c
4. d
5. d

You can take the complete Online Interactive Chapter Practice Test

for 24. Time inconsistency and health
on all key terms, persons, places, and concepts.

No Additional Costs

http://www.Cram101.com

Register, send an email request to Travis.Reese@Cram101.com to get your user Id and password.

Include your customer order number, and ISBN number from your studyguide Retailer.

Want More?
JustTheFacts101.com...

Jtf101.com provides the outlines and highlights of your textbooks, just like this e-StudyGuide, but also gives you the PRACTICE TESTS, and other exclusive study tools for all of your textbooks.

Learn More. *Just click*
http://www.JustTheFacts101.com/

CPSIA information can be obtained
at www.ICGtesting.com
Printed in the USA
BVHW09s1941131018
530029BV00002B/75/P